James Hale Bates

**Notes of a Tour in Mexico and California**

James Hale Bates

**Notes of a Tour in Mexico and California**

ISBN/EAN: 9783337327156

Printed in Europe, USA, Canada, Australia, Japan

Cover: Foto ©Andreas Hilbeck / pixelio.de

More available books at **www.hansebooks.com**

# NOTES OF A TOUR

IN

# MEXICO AND CALIFORNIA.

BY

J. H. BATES.

*PRINTED FOR PRIVATE DISTRIBUTION.*

NEW YORK:
BURR PRINTING HOUSE.
1887.

Copyright, 1887,
By J. H. BATES.

# PREFACE.

During a recent excursion with my family in the neighboring Republic of Mexico, in California and other States and Territories of our own country, I made hasty notes from day to day of what I saw, and while these convey an inadequate idea of observations whose accuracy cannot always be depended on, I have yet ventured to think that my friends and acquaintances will not dislike to read what my impressions were, since it may be said, truly perhaps, that if any one will describe with sincerity, however imperfectly it may be done, those things he has himself seen, a certain interest will attach to the performance.

With this feeling I have made a little book of these notes, and will ask those to whom I send a copy to regard it as a souvenir of the tour itself and of my cordial memory of themselves as well.

J. H. BATES.

Brooklyn, N. Y., June, 1887.

# CONTENTS.

### CHAPTER I.

*En route—An ice blockade—A magnificent fountain —Leave for Chattanooga, Tenn.—A high iron bridge—Lookout Mountain—National Cemetery— Birmingham, Ala.—Lake View—Tuscaloosa, Ala. —A pleasant ride—State Lunatic Asylum*........ 1

### CHAPTER II.

*New Orleans, La.—The French Quarter—The Old*

# ERRATA.

See p. 27. Tenth line from top should read, "In the morning" instead of evening.

See p. 50. Fourteenth line from top should read, "From October to middle of June."

# CONTENTS.

### CHAPTER I.

*En route—An ice blockade—A magnificent fountain —Leave for Chattanooga, Tenn.—A high iron bridge—Lookout Mountain—National Cemetery— Birmingham, Ala.—Lake View—Tuscaloosa, Ala. —A pleasant ride—State Lunatic Asylum* ........ 1

### CHAPTER II.

*New Orleans, La.—The French Quarter—The Old French Market—Galveston, Tex.—San Antonio, Tex.—The Alamo—The Rio Grande River—A visit to the San Philipe Spring—The Painted Cave— El Paso*............................................. 8

### CHAPTER III.

*A description of Chihuahua, Mex.—Entertained by the Governor and his wife—The Cathedral—The State House—The Town of Lerdo*.... ............ 15

### CHAPTER IV.

*Zacatecas and its quaint beauty—The Mint—Soldiers and beggars—Loafers' paradise—The village of Guadalupe—Church of Our Lady of Guadalupe— —An Orphan Asylum—Cruelty to animals*....... 21

### CHAPTER V.

*Aguas Calientes—Its baths—We experience a hot day —A dreary, dusty ride—Meet an ice-cream dealer— The City of Leon—Old customs—See a remarkable cactus—On our way to Silao*...................... 27

## CHAPTER VI.

*Arrive at Silao—Off for Marfil—A description of the Valenciana Mine—Guanajuato—Its historic interest—The Alliondiga Graneditas—What we there witnessed—Querétaro—Cerro de las Campanas—Scene of Emperor Maximilian's execution.* 33

## CHAPTER VII.

*We reach the Mexico Station of the Central Railroad—Iturbide Hotel—Paseo de la Reforma—The Alameda, or principal park—A brilliant equestrian picture—The National Theatre and Sarah Bernhardt*............................................. 41

## CHAPTER VIII.

*We visit a private museum, also Chapultepec and the Monte de Piedad, or National Pawn-shop—The Cathedral—Its grandeur and impressiveness—An inspection of the National Museum and Academy of Fine Arts—The College of Medicine—The streets and houses of Mexico—How tortilla, the national corn food, is made*........................... 47

## CHAPTER IX.

*Go to Guadalupe by tramcar—A disappointment—Legend of Our Lady of Guadalupe—The sacred spring—"The Chapel of the Well" and "The Chapel of the Little Hill"—A description of the city and of the enormous ditch Tajo de Nochistongo.* 60

## CHAPTER X.

*We attend mass at the Cathedral—The "Tree of the Dismal Night"—Toluca—Pulque and how it is made—Market-day in Toluca—The Nevado de Toluca Mountain—A grand view from the Castle of Chapultepec—Famous cypress trees—A magnificent spring of water—Tacubaya and its Observatory*..................................................... 67

CONTENTS.   vii

## CHAPTER XI.

*We visit the Methodist Church—Dine at the Concordia Restaurant—Witness a bull-fight—A description of the repulsive scenes there enacted* ..... 76

## CHAPTER XII.

*A "Norther" and its result—A ride to Apizaco—We see a pretty bit of scenery—San Juan Teotihuacan and its two ancient pyramids—A brilliant view of Ixtaccihuatl and Popocatapetl—Puebla and what we saw there* ..... 86

## CHAPTER XIII.

*A ride to Cholula and something about it and its pyramid—The Franciscan Monastery—Pleasant cogitations—We set off for Tlascala and visit its Governor—The old Church of San Francisco—The descent to the Tierras Calientes—We linger at Orizaba and enjoy its many beauties—Start for Mexico City—A fine view of the Southern Cross* .. 92

## CHAPTER XIV.

*The Iturbide Hotel and its cheerlessness—A chilly day—A paragraph about the bull-fight—A visit to the Cathedral and a description of its interior and its devotees—Take leave of Mexico with a few remarks on its past and present government—A ride through many places of interest* ..... 102

## CHAPTER XV.

*We pass an enjoyable day at the Hotel Raymond—Take a long drive to the Sunny Slope Winery—"Lucky Baldwin" and his ranch—We visit Los Angeles and then ride to "Kinneyloar," the residence of a retired New York cigarette-maker—Leave for 'Frisco—Golden Gate Park—A drive through Chinatown* ..... 113

## CHAPTER XVI.

*The Cliff House—Sea-lions and their haunts—A sight of Chinatown at night—Its streets, its shops, and* the character of its inhabitants—The opium dens—Go to a Chinese theatre and witness a performance, after which we enter a Joss-house and make observations .................................................. 121

## CHAPTER XVII.

*Arrive at Monterey—Go to the Hotel del Monte and see its famous park—Leave for Santa Cruz—The big trees—A good climate for invalids—Napa, and the Napa Soda Springs Hotel—The charming Napa Valley—A ride to the Geysers—We describe them—Something about Charley Foss, the whip* ....... 131

## CHAPTER XVIII.

*Bound for home—Stop on our way at Sacramento, where we are entertained by the city—Off again, and after travelling through miles of country of varied scenery, change at Ogden, and enter Salt Lake City—Description of the city, and a few words about the Mormons and their peculiar institutions* .................................................. 141

## CHAPTER XIX.

*A beautiful morning—Attend service in the Congregational Church—Liberty of speech and some specimens—A visit to the Tabernacle—We describe its services, and make a few observations on polygamy and show how it can be abolished* .................... 149

## CHAPTER XX.

*Leave Salt Lake City for Provo—Castle Gate and Cliffs—Pass through Gunnison and cross the Rocky Mountains—View the wonders of the Grand Cañon of the Arkansas—Manitou Springs—The "Garden of the Gods"—The grave of Helen Hunt—Denver—The mining regions—Meet with a railroad accident—A wait, when we have time to see the antics of a "bucking broncho"—Off again—Nearing home—Pleasant cogitations—Home at Last* ............ 158

# A TOUR IN MEXICO AND CALIFORNIA.

## CHAPTER 1.

*En route—An ice blockade—A magnificent fountain—Leave for Chattanooga, Tenn.—A high iron bridge—Lookout Mountain—National Cemetery—Birmingham, Ala.—Lake View—Tuscaloosa, Ala.—A pleasant ride—State Lunatic Asylum.*

*January* 31*st*, 1887.—Left Jersey City by New York, Lake Erie and Western Railroad at 9 A.M., to join a Raymond excursion party leaving Boston at 2 P.M. to-day for Mexico and California. My party consists of wife, daughter Betty, and niece Mary. Day clear and pleasant. No snow visible until beyond Paterson, then only in patches for miles further. At Lackawanna the Delaware and Hudson Canal is carried across the Delaware River from the left to the right bank in an aqueduct bridge. Fifty miles further up found the river "gorged" with ice—said to be the worst in a great many years. The river is not dammed up in any one place, but is so filled with floating ice for a long way that the mass and weight of it impede and delay the water until it rises and spreads, taking the movable ice with it and doing much damage for a wide distance on both banks. A poor man at one point was moving his family and goods from his house by boat. In some places the current had quite left its old bed, being forced out by the ice.

Reached Hornellsville at 7 P.M. in a snow-storm, and passed the night at the Osborn House.

*February 1st.*—Raymond train took us up at 10.30 A.M., being an hour late. At Salamanca the train entered on the New York, Pennsylvania and Ohio Railroad, now a part of the system of the Erie. Here the time changes from Eastern to Central, one hour slower. All through the oil regions in the neighborhood of Jamestown, Corry, and Meadville are thousands of huge tanks for storing the oil for the pipe lines. Passed through Akron, O., in the evening, and Sterling, Mansfield, Urbana, Springfield, and Dayton during the night, entering at the last-named town on the Cleveland, Columbus, Cincinnati and Indianapolis Railroad, a part of the " Bee Line," and reach Cincinnati at 9 A.M.

*February 2d.*—A very heavy rain with thunder and lightning all through the day. Good rooms at the Gibson House. Our Raymond tickets include everything, and rooms are assigned on reaching a hotel. Drove with wife to a dentist, and on the way admired, not for the first time, the fountain presented to the city by Mr. Henry Probasco, a wealthy citizen. This magnificent fountain, among the finest in the world, consists mainly of a colossal female of bronze nine feet in height, standing on a highly-wrought bronze pedestal, about whose base is spread a broad basin of Bavarian porphyry. The figure is majestic, in flowing robes, looking down from a height of forty-three feet, with an expression of sweet benignity, while from her outstretched palms, extended as in the act of blessing, the water falls in showery mists. It would not seem easy to set forth the beautiful use of water in a more charming and impressive way than is here done by Von Kreling of Nuremberg, son-in-law of the great Kaulbach, aided by Von Miller, the director of the royal bronze foundry of Bavaria at Munich, where the parts of the fountain were cast from bronze obtained from cannon bought of the Danish Government. The cost was considerably over one hundred thousand dollars, and is a fine instance of what a public-spirited citizen can do to beautify his own city. What a magnificent city New York would be if only a not large part of her greatly rich citizens would find their satisfaction in thus adorning it; and if one is emulous of an honorable name, how can he better secure it than by rearing in everlasting brass a monument of such beauty and utility to all classes of his fellow-citizens as shall bring his name constantly to their lips in blessing?

In the evening had a doctor to Betty, who was sick all night; but able to resume the road in the morning.

*February 3d.*—Left at 9 A.M. for Chattanooga by the Cincinnati and Southern Division of the Queen and Crescent Route. One hundred miles out crossed the Kentucky River on an iron bridge two hundred and seventy-six feet above the water. The river runs through a cañon of almost that depth cut by the river through strata of limestone; often the alternate one being black from some cause, perhaps taking a deeper color from the weather, so that these long, uniform layers of alternate black and gray are strikingly like artificial and ornamental masonry. Further on is a similar bridge one hundred feet above the Cumberland. The uncommon rains and the weight of our train—seven Pullman cars and a baggage car—led to caution in running, so that we did not reach Chattanooga until 3 A.M., instead of 11 P.M., the schedule time.

*February 4th.*—Lived in our sleeping and dining cars left outside of station. Rode to top of Lookout Mountain, sixteen hundred feet above the Tennessee River. The air was thick, but clear enough to show that the view is beautiful and grand. There has been much rubbish written about the fighting on Lookout Mountain. Hooker was sent against a Confederate force on the mountain top and sides, as one of the incidental movements in Grant's strategy that day, the real object being to coax Bragg to send troops from Missionary Ridge. This he did, and Grant moved on his main army and defeated it. Any one can see that no sort of military movements is possible on the upper half of the mountain. "Hooker among the clouds," and all that, was a good deal the work of the glowing war correspondent of the period.

In the well-kept National Cemetery here lie buried nearly thirteen thousand slain in the several battles hereabout, including the disastrous field of Chickamauga. The name of every Northern State appears on the white headstones, that of Michigan and others being repeated over and over.

Left for Birmingham, Ala., 10 P.M.

*February 5th.*—Woke at 7 A.M. at the station in Birmingham. Rode, at the invitation of Major W. J. Milnes, Secretary and Treasurer of the Elyton Land Co., on train drawn by a dummy-engine to Lake View, a suburb some three miles direct from the centre of the town, with small hills and ravines—a pretty enough region, where are a good many rather fine cottages and some agreeable effects of landscape-gardening, a good deal of it being the work of the Elyton Land Co., a concern of much enterprise which has made money by booming real estate here. This town would seem to have a bright future. Certainly it now appears extremely prosperous. It has come on in less than ten years from an insignificant hamlet to a population of thirty thousand or more, and is well built, largely of brick in the business parts. The interests are chiefly iron and coal in proximity in the immediate neighborhood, in great abundance—red hematite and brown ores—so that it is claimed that even now, with much that is crude in the processes, pig iron is made at about two thirds the cost of the same in Pennsylvania.

Left for Tuscaloosa, 2 P.M. An arrangement had been made, ostensibly by the Mayor of the town, to give the entire party a carriage-ride and show the town, and let the world know that it, as well as other points in the South now waking up and getting themselves talked about, has merits too, and a future, if only somebody will take it in hand. Probably land-owners and speculators paid the cost of thirty to forty of the most ancient and diseased vehicles now extant. 'Twas a kindly deed though, whoever did it, and we enjoyed a ride through and around what I should judge to be a typical Southern inland town, little changed from ante-bellum days, unless more forlorn and decayed. The population is said to be thirty-five hundred, and it was once the capital of Alabama, the melancholy, huge structure wherein the wisdom of the State used to assemble being converted into a Baptist school. It is also the seat of the State University, whose students are called cadets and wear a gray uniform. Here, too, is the State Lunatic Asylum, where our whole party, making a dismal procession, as if returning from the funeral of some popular judge or colonel, were " unloaded," as the person in charge expressed it, and taken through such parts of the commodious and well-kept building as Dr. Bryce, the courteous physician in charge, permitted. Dr. Bryce is said to stand high in his specialty, and informed us that no restraint is used upon the inmates.

# CHAPTER II.

*New Orleans, La.—The French Quarter—The Old French Market—Galveston, Tex.—San Antonio, Tex.—The Alamo—The Rio Grande River—A visit to the San Philipe Spring—The Painted Cave—El Paso.*

*February 6th.*—Reached New Orleans, eighteen hundred and forty-eight miles from New York, at 6 A.M., and went direct to the St. Charles. Found letters here. Walked at length through the French Quarter. In the evening heard Dr. Palmer, of the First Presbyterian Church, preach—an able man of the Old School of faith.

*February 7th.*—Went through the old French Market. Its quaintness, etc., about which much has been written, is greatly overrated. The buildings are a series of commonplace sheds, something like those built on to the old Fulton Market, without the slightest interest in any way. Rode in the afternoon through the best parts of the city. The impressions I formed two years ago when here are confirmed. While there are a good many fine residences, the city, on the whole, has a poor look. The war is said to have greatly injured it, and no doubt its relative importance was once greater in commerce and fashion; but the population as a whole would seem never to have been prosperous. The mercury was seventy degrees at 2 P.M.

This makes a strong contrast with Brooklyn—a contrast enhanced by the rich green of trees and shrubs along the best streets, where pains have been taken to rear them. We saw no flowers out of doors. In the markets saw nearly all the fresh vegetables we get at home in the summer, cabbages, onions, beets, tomatoes, squash, potatoes, and some others not usual with us, and several varieties of fish—the red-snapper and pompino, of which I ate, being excellent.

*February 8th.*—Left New Orleans for the City of Mexico at 11 A.M., by the Southern Pacific Railroad's Southern route, crossing the Mississippi by ferry to Algiers. Took special train made up for the Raymond party of new Pullman cars which have made only one trip before—that to California and return. There are of the Mexican train three sleepers, a dining and baggage car. Crossed a low, rich, alluvial land growing sugar-cane, the Bayou Têche region, including New Iberia, specially to be noted. Weather warm, not less than seventy-five degrees, and sky and air and earth summery. Heard frogs in free chorus at bed-time. Woke at Houston in the vast State of Texas, within whose borders we travel nearly a thousand miles.

*February 9th.*—Train ran down to Galveston for five hours, then returned to Houston and the direct road. Galveston has a population of say thirty thousand; is on an island between Galveston Bay on one side and the Gulf of Mexico on the other. The railroad bridge on piles over the bay is two miles long. The town is fairly well built on a sand-bed, slightly above the level of the water, so that rain-water is saved in huge tuns as in New Orleans, is busy-looking, and seems, from the considerable shipping in the harbor, to do a good trade by water. The beach on the Gulf side is of firm, fine sand, and forms a capital driveway. Vegetation is hard to get, as the site of the city is only deep, fine sand. Almost the only growth resembling a tree I saw is the completest possible caricature of nature—a distorted trunk, grotesque and dismal to the last degree, with thwarted, stunted branches and a ridiculous imitation of leafage, called "salt-water cedar."

*February 10th.*—Woke near San Antonio. First saw cactus growing wild. All the plant life is new to me. The grass—now dry—is fine and thick. The *mesquité*—between a shrub and tree in size—*chaparral,* sage-brush, cat's-claw, live-oak, and a small variety, new also to me, called pin-oak, were all the vegetation I saw for miles. San Antonio is an old town, has lately taken a start, and claims thirty thousand population. I should think this a liberal estimate. Good modern business and dwelling houses mix with small, mean *adobé* structures and others built of a very friable conglomerate much used in early times and easily affected even by the comparatively mild weather here. The streets are narrow, and the plaza, with the old Alamo on it, gives a foreign air to the place. It was in this structure of stone that, in the struggle for Texan independence, Santa Aña with four thousand men besieged and cruelly slaughtered with particulars of atrocity a little band of Texans, one hundred and forty-four in number, including Travis, Bowie (the inventor of the Bowie-knife), and the still more famous David Crockett. The State has assumed charge of this building, and maintains a custodian in it, who fights over again the battles of both sides, with many incidents, I fear, which never occurred to the participants. At the State capital, too, is a monument with the inscription, "Thermopylæ had its messenger of defeat; the Alamo had none"—a neat way of saying that all were destroyed.

Drove three miles from town to the source of River San Antonio, here about the size—somewhat larger—than, say, the Black River at Cavendish, Vt. It begins from two issues of water directly from the ground, some-half mile apart, and nearly equal in volume. These unite and form the river, which is thus full-born at once. Drove, after dinner at Menger House, to the remains of the Mission Churches of La Concepcion and San Juan, four miles from the city. These are, say, one hundred and fifty years old, and were originally well built, but by reason of the softness of the stone used are in ruins. There is a pretty tree cultivated on the streets called "china berry," quite new to me. There are as yet no signs of spring here in the vegetation.

Left for El Paso at 3 A.M., lying at the station until then.

*February 11th.*—Woke thirty to forty miles from Del Rio on the Rio Grande, separating the United States from Mexico. Visited a spring called San Philipe, which pours from the ground in a volume equal to the Black River at Plymouth Pond, Vt., transparent and pure to look and taste, much finer than the sources of the San Antonio. Followed the Rio Grande up for, say, fifty miles—a muddy yellow stream of about the volume of the San Antonio at the city of that name, flowing through deep cuts of limestone, where is a cavity in a cliff called the Painted Cave, reached by steeply climbing some thirty feet to the entrance. This cavern is about thirty feet high, sixty wide, and seventy-five deep. High up on the rear wall in one place is a considerable space picked out in red ochre into a small set design, not unlike some of those seen on Indian dressed buffalo-robes, whence its name. Just under this painted bit is a small spring of dubious water. From the front of this cavern one can look across the river to the smooth-cut, precipitous layers of limestone, so level and uniform in thickness that they seem like the massive masonry of man's work, extending as far as the eye can reach up and down the Mexican side—a stage and auditorium fit for the old gods to enact a play. Just beyond we crossed the Pecos River, a tributary of the Rio Grande. The country all day has been the picture of desolation. The mercury, eighty degrees at 2 P.M., under the influence of a "Norther," went down to fifty-five degrees at 5 P.M.

*February 12th.*—Woke ninety miles from El Paso, where the train lies until 5 P.M. Here baggage is examined by the Mexican customs, and we cross the Rio Grande into Mexico. This town, twelve hundred miles from New

Orleans, is growing rapidly, and has come from a dull Mexican hamlet, in five years, to a smart city, with streets, a number of substantial brick buildings, and a growing importance from the concentration of railroads here, Santa Fé, Southern Pacific, and Mexican Central. The country over which we have passed since leaving San Antonio is for the most part arid and desolate. Trueheart, one of the interpreters of the party, born in San Antonio, and quite well informed, states that the soil away from the river, which we followed all day yesterday, is better, but that a large part of Texas is barren for want of water—so fatally wanting. Water has to be carried to the stations away from the river in trains made on purpose—huge, rectangular boxes, water-tight. Stories are told of cattle coming a hundred miles to water, and dying at a terrible rate for want of it.

Left El Paso at 7 P.M. Saw a memorable sunset from El Paso del Norte on the Mexican side of the Rio Grande—the sky opaline and a rare violet tint on the low, serrated, and desolate hills at the west. Our Raymond cars were attached to the regular Mexican Central train to Chihuahua, thence to have their own engine to the City of Mexico, distant twelve hundred and twenty-five miles directly south-east.

# CHAPTER III.

*A description of Chihuahua, Mex.—Entertained by the Governor and his wife—The Cathedral—The State House—The Town of Lerdo.*

*February* 13*th.*—Woke at Chihuahua, two hundred and twenty-four miles from El Paso, and looked down to the west from the train on the picture of a town and surroundings so utterly unlike anything I have ever seen that, were I told we were in Palestine or Egypt, all about me would confirm it. In the midst of an arid plain, surrounded by low scarped ranges and detached swells and peaks of hills all about, lies a city of, say, fifteen thousand, with narrow streets, houses of whitewashed *adobé*, mostly one-story high, with moving forms of man, woman, and beast, unlike anything to which we are accustomed. The Rio Chubisca flows through it. Little donkeys called *burros* are seen everywhere loaded heavily with firewood of *mesquité*, cut stove-length, or bundles of wheat-straw used for fodder, and various other loads. These sturdy, patient little beasts seem to be the universal conveyance here. The Mexican with his broad-brimmed *sombrero* and many-hued *scrapé*, and the woman with her mantilla or *rebozo*, present, in the atmosphere and background here, figures exceedingly picturesque. The houses are low, and closely shut with barred windows on the street, but those of the better sort open into quite spacious courts with stone stairways leading up to a balcony running all round, on which open the doors of the upper apartments in houses of more than one story.

We called on the Governor of this State of Chihuahua, Felix Francisco Macaya, a banker, and were admitted into a paved court through a strong double door opening in the solid wall directly from the street. In the centre of this court were some growing plants, and all about doors opening into various apartments. The Governor's wife received us with great politeness, and at once proceeded to show us through some rooms used as sleeping-rooms, etc., taking us for that purpose through a small apartment where we saw a number of young people, sons and daughters and other relatives, to whom we were introduced; after which she led the way to the parlor, followed by all the family, some of whom at once went to the piano and sang a song in Spanish to an old air. There was a harsh burr in their voices that I have noticed in another case of a Mexican songstress. On retiring we all shook hands with much cordiality.

Had at breakfast in our dining-car fruit of an oval shape, the size of a goose-egg, with rough, green rind, called *chirrimoya*, tasting somewhat like the banana.

The Cathedral, built of sandstone, begun in 1737, is said to have cost eight hundred thousand dollars, which was raised by a special tax of one real (twelve and a half cents) in each eight dollars on the yield of the Santa Eulalia silver mines in the neighboring mountains. Mr. John R. Robinson, who married a Miss Taylor, of Brooklyn, is now the owner of them. Called on him in the evening. He says the mines are over two hundred years old and had yielded when he took them about three hundred million dollars. In the plaza is a handsome fountain, and after dark a military band played there, not very well, and on the promenade about it a good part of the people—common enough they are—walked in the sufficient light of the paraffine lamps set on posts.

Attended church in the morning at a mission of the Congregational Church, under the auspices of the Boston Board, in charge of Rev. James Eaton. 'Tis the old story of missions. Although all things favor, there are but thirty-four members, as Mr. Eaton counts them, and those of the humblest and poorest. He stated that those who left the Catholic faith to join him sacrificed their means of living and became social outcasts. Surely those who lead these or any other people to desert the faith of their fathers, when the consequences are so serious, assume a grave responsibility, which only the fullest belief in Calvinism can warrant any one in undertaking. These converts had before been baptized into a faith in Christ and were professors in the Catholic Church. It is therefore to convert them to a different body of doctrine that these missions are set up.

In the rear of the State House, a fine building of stone, stands a monument on the spot where Miguel Hidalgo, curate of Dolores, and one of his companions, Captain Allende, were executed July 31st, 1811. He was the brave and patriotic priest who in 1810 began the movement for liberating his country from Spain, and his name is held in veneration all over the republic, as that of Washington is with us.

*February* 14*th.*—Left at 7 A.M. for Zacatecas, distant four hundred and seventeen miles. For two hundred miles the road continues through the State of Chihuahua, then enters Northwestern Durango, then later on South-western Coahuila. The whole route is across a broad, level plain, with mountain-ranges always in sight on either hand. These have local names, but are really continuations of the great ranges of the

Rocky and Sierra Nevada Mountains, forming the backbone of the northern part of the Mexican plateau, and flattened down as it were into a vast plain, beginning in New Mexico and extending down to the City of Mexico, leaving spurs and distinct short ranges and separate peaks, often of fantastic forms, notched and incised to a degree unknown in the mountains of our Northern States, and utterly destitute of vegetation. Far as the eye can reach, except at infrequent intervals, the soil is parched, brown, or rather gray, and devoid of other vegetation than the unsightly cacti, with here and there a stunted *mesquité* tree, or rather shrub.

After nearly three hundred miles of this sort of country, we reach Lerdo, a town in the Laguna section or the Mapimi Basin, where is the inestimable boon of water, so that the water-trains from which our engine has been supplied at different points can be replenished. Here, too, is a region of considerable extent, where cotton, sugar-cane, corn, and wheat are grown. This fertile land is mostly in two immense farms called *haciendas*, owned by two Spaniards. We crossed the beds of no less than six streams of importance in the rainy season, but now dry as a bone. The most important of these is the Nazas, which by the first of July will be filled with water coming, it is said, from mountains three hundred miles away. Then, as with all running water here, this will be drawn into long ditches and ponds and saved for irrigating the fields. Not only is there not a navigable river in all the vast Mexican plateau, but, I am informed, scarcely one which does not disappear during the dry season, extending, as a rule, through nine months in the year. The rainy season begins about the middle of June and continues, in variable quantities, for a period of about ten weeks; then follow all the rest of the year cloudless skies and a blazing sun.

# CHAPTER IV.

*Zacatecas and its quaint beauty—The Mint—Soldiers and beggars—Loafers' paradise—The village of Guadalupe—Church of Our Lady of Guadalupe—An Orphan Asylum—Cruelty to animals.*

*February 15th.*—Woke at Zacatecas, eighty-two hundred feet above the sea-level. Said to have a population of forty thousand. Went up into the city from the station by tramway. The city is the capital of the State of the same name and the centre of one of the richest mining districts in the republic. It is crowded in the most picturesque way into a narrow ravine, and has had the title of a city since 1585. The hills all about are honeycombed with silver mines and afford magnificent views. I did not think it possible that anywhere could be such absolute strangeness in everything as here. One might be in the remotest part of the East. Our painters go to Tangier and the distant Orient for subjects. Judging from what they bring back, one would say that here on every hand are subjects fully equal—mellow, quaint bits, whole streets of the style brought into Spain by the Moors, filled with picturesque figures, unique beyond expression. In the midst of the plaza is a fountain with a huge basin of stone, from which the entire population carries its drinking-water in earthen jars like those used in the East three thousand years ago.

Called at the Mint, where the decimal silver is coining; also on the Bishop of Zacatecas, José Maria Refugio Guerra y Alva, whose residence, in the Moorish style, is delightful, with its cool, cheerful court of stone, on which opens the balcony running all around, with flowers in pots set in iron loops fitted into its railings. The bishop is a kindly and rather intellectual-looking man, of fine presence, who received us cordially in a well-arranged reception-room opening from a large library of many books.

The Cathedral did not much interest me. High up on the wall on one side is a niche with a little penthouse roof over it, where is a nearly life-size image of the Crucifixion in colors now dull, having in the wounds huge artificial roses. The minutely carved front is a combination of Christian and Aztec art.

Close beside the Cathedral is a barracks with many soldiers on duty or lounging about in white uniforms; and on the flagging of the little plaza in front huge stone seats, where a lot of sturdy beggars, in the most picturesque of parti-colored rags, sat under the blazing sun, in dirt and dignity, much like the "gray-back senators" on the benches in front of the New York City Hall. I noticed that a number of them had under their arms a stick of green sugar-cane about two feet long, and when the great Cathedral clock struck noon they fell to biting and sucking these for luncheon.

This land is loafers' paradise—little clothing, little food, and less shelter being needed. The people here, beggars and all, seem to have good muscles, healthy flesh, and a mildly happy look, as if the scanty supply of all that we consider essential to comfort quite satisfied them. The water supplying the only fountain of drinking-water is brought a mile in an open aqueduct of stone, arched in places. The well or spring furnishing the water has a huge wheel revolving in it, moved by mule-power, on the rim of which are little tin buckets. These empty themselves into the aqueduct. The whole is of the most primitive sort. The mules were feeding when I was at the well, and the wheel at rest, on the movement of which depended the very life of forty thousand souls. I never realized the force and beauty of the many beautiful allusions to the element of water in the poetical books of the Old Testament as here in this arid land. The pressing eagerness with which the people, young and old, of both sexes and all conditions, crowded about the great fountain in the plaza, and bent over the brim, dipping up the precious fluid into all sorts of vessels, and hurrying away as if in the little *adobe* houses life or death was depending on its coming speedily, is exceedingly interesting to one from a land and conditions such as make water, so common is it, almost the least regarded of life's common blessings.

Lunched in our dining-car as usual; then took tramway to the village of Guadalupe, five miles distant from here. Here is a pleasant garden set with oleanders, acacias, and roses, whose long vines are twined into arbors. Here is a costly and beautiful chapel to Our Lady of Guadalupe, the patron saint of Mexico, erected and completed three years ago by Señora Dominga Marie Miranda, widow of Señor Miranda, owner of the San Rafael silver mines. It is said to have cost two hundred thousand dollars, which, taking into account the cheapness of the principal material (the sandstone of the walls) and the low price of labor (fifty cents per day), would equal, I should think, three hundred thousand dollars in the States. It is of small size, of handsome proportions, and thickly overlaid with gold-leaf, covering, I think, not less than one quarter of the entire interior. The dome is specially rich and fine. It is said to be the finest church in Mexico, and our interpreters on the train believe it the finest in the world. It adjoins a church dedicated also to Our Lady, built by the Jesuits in 1721. This is a rich interior, with its ceiling of carved arabesques. Attached to the church is an Orphan Asylum, the most important charity in Mexico, founded in 1875 by General Trinidad Gorcia de la Cadena, where over one thousand orphans are maintained and educated in school and in the trades. We heard a band play several airs, all the performers being orphans, and play them well.

They manufacture here the striped Mexican blanket called *serapé*. I bought one for two dollars and eighty cents, Mexican money, equal to two dollars and ten cents of ours.

The cars ran down from Zacatecas by the force of gravity, and were drawn back by six mules, harnessed three abreast, and belabored unmercifully all the way by the driver and an extra man who seemed there on purpose to rest the driver, who had two heavy, cruel whips —one long lash for the leaders and a shorter for the wheelers. These he changed often, but kept one or the other going on the poor beasts, sometimes passing one to his assistant when he wanted to make a special burst of speed. The usual pace was a gallop. This cruel whipping of the mules seemed to make no impression upon them — indeed, it seems to be a part of their regular treatment, and done by force of habit; for the driver kept mauling the mule nearest him, without the slightest reference to his work. The wanton cruelty of those who have to do with animals in this country is shocking. These car-drivers will give a cruel blow to a donkey standing idly by the carway; and ours, on one of the trips, struck a pig in mere wantonness such a blow as stunned the poor wretch till we were out of reach.

Mr. Wells, the agent of Wells & Fargo here, stated that they ship seven million dollars a year of silver from this point, the product of the mines hereabouts. One owned by General Escabado, the Vita Grande, is said to pay two thousand dollars per share per month.

Returning through the village, a confused blending of many childish voices was heard issuing from the open windows of a low-roofed *adobé* house fronting the street, proceeding as we found from a school for children, all the pupils being engaged in studying their lessons aloud.

Quaint Zacatecas! It does not seem to me that I shall see anything here or in another land to impress me so much as I have been impressed by thee in my inexperience of foreign lands. Left at 6 P.M.

## CHAPTER V.

*Aguas Calientes—Its baths—We experience a hot day—A dreary, dusty ride—Meet an ice-cream dealer—The City of Leon—Old customs—See a remarkable cactus—On our way to Silao.*

*February 16th.*—Woke at Aguas Calientes, seventy-five miles nearer the City of Mexico. This city is said to have a population of twenty thousand, and is fair to see from the station. In the evening we went to the baths near by, housed in a large enclosure of high stone walls. The baths are on two sides of a rectangle, the larger ones opening from an inner wall into an anteroom giving, through a Moorish arch, on a pool of pure warm water open to the sky, about fourteen by twelve feet, and four feet deep. The walls of stone, painted in dull red, are crenellated at the top. Such baths, I suppose, as the Moors introduced into Spain. The water comes from a famous hot spring a mile away, conveyed by an earthen pipe underground, and by the time it gets to these baths is about eighty degrees Fahrenheit and delicious to the feel. The waste water flows away to irrigate the fields. There are, in fact, two of these springs near each other, one being used at first by the city for baths, then flowing a long way in an open ditch, in which men, women, and children were bathing together, some quite naked, and all along women washing clothes.

A hot day. Mercury eighty-nine in the car at 4 P.M. Ice taken on the train here from Popocatapetl, in pieces six inches thick, wrapped in straw. A peripatetic dealer in ice-cream appeared with a tub on his shoulder, the cream in little tin tubes three inches long and one inch in diameter. Bought one of these at the station and tasted. Tasted only, and then passed it to a delicate Spanish woman with two slender children, waiting for the train, and received a grateful look from her large, dark, melancholy eyes, so frequent here. The vendor explained that his ice—in little plates—was got by laying a leaf of the *maguey* on the ground and pouring a thin depth of water on it. This by evaporation and chill of the night air he insists forms a thin coat of ice, which he puts away in the ground.

All went to the plaza in the town in the evening, where the military band of the Seventh Cavalry played for an hour. The band of the Eighth I heard at the Exposition in New Orleans, and it was said to be the best, but I was told here that in a competition the Seventh took the medal. I should not approve the finding.

*February 17th.*—Left Aguas Calientes at 5 A.M. for Leon, one hundred and five miles away. Thirty miles out the railroad is carried over the Rio Encarnacion on a fine bridge one hundred and fifty feet above the stream. Thirty-nine miles further on is Lagos, a town of thirteen thousand inhabitants, and one of the points of departure from the railroad to Guadalajara, the capital of Jalisco, one hundred and thirty miles, or two days by diligence. One of these dreary carriages, with its six mules harnessed three abreast, stood waiting at the station, coated thickly, inside and outside, with fine gray dust.

With few exceptions the roads of the republic are described as in dreadful condition; and a long ride in one of these big coaches, built in Troy, N. Y., under a blazing sun, choked with a cloud of ever-present dust, and tossed back and forth from seat to roof as the mules gallop madly along to the loud shouts and perpetual flogging of the muleteers, is said to be a torture so excruciating that only the direst necessity will compel any one to adventure it the second time.

Signor Riveroll, our chief interpreter, stated that ice would form last night on the *maguey* leaf, and showed me, as we drew near Leon at 10 A.M., a great number of these leaves, also shallow earthen dishes set on the ground for ice, forming in the way described above. Most excellent oranges—the finest I have ever eaten—come to the stations in huge circular baskets of straw, brought on the backs of *burros* a long way over the mountains.

Rode by tramway from the station to Leon, the second largest city of Mexico, of say seventy-five thousand souls. It has. an *Alameda*, or garden and promenade, set with ash trees bordered with dressed stone. Leon is in the midst of a plain of great extent, differing from any land we have yet seen by having water near the surface, and so being only partly dependent on irrigation. This plain is of great fertility, called almost the richest in the republic, and extends, with brief interruptions, to the City of Mexico. The station agent said it has been worked one hundred and fifty years without fertilizing. We saw in the market and had at dinner on our dining-car, the "Raymond," the most delicious lettuce, grown here. Saw men watering the streets with water brought from a ditch near by in great earthen pots ; also all along water being drawn as the Egyptians did and do, by a rude " sweep." The wells are not more than three to four feet deep.

There are many species of cactus, some growing to a prodigious size. On the way to Leon by tramcar I saw a stem of what is called the organ cactus, rising not less than thirty feet perpendicularly. This remarkable plant has a single straight stem made up of parts several feet long, six-sided, and joined so as to make one perfect trunk, with joints hardly visible. The larger ones here are six inches in diameter. They plant them side by side and make a fence as connected as could be done by driving stakes into the ground close together. Another species grows like a tree, with branches and a dark rind, looking, a little way off, exactly like a large fruit-tree, fully as big in trunk and limbs as any apple-tree on Brook Farm.

Was not much impressed with Leon, whose principal features seemed tame after romantic Zacatecas. Leather goods are extensively manufactured here—boots and saddles, shoes, and the *huaraches*, or leathern sandals, worn by the poorer classes and mostly by the soldiers, and preferred in this warm climate to close boots or shoes. The blue *rebozos*, or long, narrow shawls universally worn by the women, are extensively made here; but, on the whole, Leon is an uninteresting city to the tourist.

At 2 P.M. came on to Silao, twenty miles further, a place of no special interest, and remained all night, always in our sleeping-car. Here is a flouring-mill said to have been running for one hundred years, in the hands of one family. The old way was to put the grain on a threshing-floor and trample it out with mules, then winnow it by hand, as in Bible times, then wash it and grind by mules. Lately steam-power has been brought in, and the wood used is bought by the pound and brought to market, as everything is, on the backs of the little *burros*. There were two piles of this precious article visible in the mill-yard from the station, about as large as would keep both families at Brook Farm for a year, and the station agent said it was reckoned worth about twenty thousand dollars.

A military band came to the train and played for an hour.

## CHAPTER VI.

*Arrive at Silao—Off for Marfil—A description of the Valenciana Mine—Guanajuato—Its historic interest—The Alliondiga Graneditas—What we there witnessed –Querétaro—Cerro de las Campanas—Scene of Emperor Maximilian's execution.*

*February* 18*th.*—Woke at 6 A.M. at Silao. At 8 A.M. took branch of the Central Road—still keeping our own train—to Marfil, a suburb of Guanajuato, capital of the State of the same name, fifteen miles from Silao, nine hundred and twenty-six feet above it, and sixty-eight hundred feet above the sea ; population seventy-five thousand ; founded 1554 ; built in a steep ravine, and one of the leading mining towns of Mexico, where is the Valenciana Mine, said to have yielded eight hundred million dollars in silver. It is reached by tramway from Marfil, being situated, like most Mexican cities, a distance from the railway-station. The tramway is laid through a rocky cañon in which is bare room for the little Rio Guanajuato and the road, and all along, at irregular heights on the hillsides, and clinging to them as if they grew there, are rows, one above another, of *adobé* or stone houses and mills, with a church with blue or yellow or dark red dome in sight at every turn. We passed a Mexican leading a *burro* whose weight could not be more than three hundred pounds, with a live fat pig, weighing certainly not less, strapped on his back crosswise, trudging to market.

All at once we are in the heart of a city swarming with life. There are some fifty works here for the reduction of the ore, most of them from two hundred to three hundred years old and adding greatly to the mediæval quaintness of the town, which is beyond description, and far surpasses anything yet seen. These " Reduction" works were originally built to repel robbers, and have walls and quaint towers pierced for musketry. The old houses rise rank above rank on the steep mountain-sides, the ground being terraced out to give room, so that it cost eighty thousand dollars, it is said, to make space for the Jesuit Church, costing two hundred thousand dollars. Narrow causeways paved with cobbles climb tortuously up at all angles among low stone houses with barred windows, painted, some blue, some dull red, some yellow, some white, and often a sort of dado of contrasting colors runs along, a dozen together, as high up as the window-ledges. Between the bars of the windows are seen the flashing black eyes, nut-brown faces, and raven hair of the women, and leaning against the walls outside hundreds of swarthy men in almost as savage garb as the Comanche Indians, looking like the bandits of story. Stairways in many places connect one terrace with another. On the terraces, in the upper portion of the city, are exceedingly handsome residences of rich citizens, with beautiful gardens along the reservoirs.

Near the city is obtained a fine variegated sandstone, blue, pale green, chocolate, and other colors, mingling in a charming way, and now used largely for building the better houses. The great want of the town is water, and at the few places where it is doled out by officers appointed for the purpose were long rows of women patiently waiting with earthen jars for their turn to fill. Most of the mines are supplied from one well, the water being pumped, as at Zacatecas, in similar quaint towers. The water-carriers here have a peculiar jar, a sort of cylinder four feet long, strapped on their backs.

Such bits of architecture and color everywhere!—the Spain of three hundred years ago, with picturesque Mexican Indians in place of Moors. The place has an historic interest. The brave Hidalgo, priest and patriot, who raised the standard of revolt from Spain, laid siege to the Spanish forces on the hills hereabouts and captured the Alliondiga Graneditas, or exchange, whither they had retreated. The town was recaptured by the Spaniards, and the head of Hidalgo, put to death at Chihuahua, was sent on here and affixed to the wall high up. The hook is pointed out to which it was affixed. The Graneditas was used, under the viceroys here and in other large towns, for those bringing crops to market to expose them for sale to the poor, forty-eight hours, at wholesale prices, before selling them to the dealers. This is now used as a prison, and we passed through a large court where near a hundred prisoners were strolling about or standing against the walls in the sun or sitting on the tiled floors, a few braiding rushes. They are prisoners of this State, corresponding to convicts of our State prisons. Their cells open from the balconies on the second story surrounding the court, and are large rooms—as large, in fact, as many of the sole rooms of the first floor of the *adobe* houses—and are filled, if need be, with as many as can lie on mats spread on the stone floor, the only light and ventilation being through two holes in the door, each say four by two inches. From the upper balcony we went by a narrow stairway to the roof, whence is a fine view of the city.

Some scenes below, fit for a place in Dante's hell, are the inclosures of several Reduction Houses, where, in accordance with the old usage since the mines were opened, some ten mules were moving slowly about in each, under a hot sun, in a sticky bed of paste made of the ore mixed with water and quicksilver, a Mexican standing in the centre plying his heavy whip without rest on these miserable brutes, wallowing on with difficulty, making a picture of misery, pain, and despair. The mercury softens the feet of the mules, so that they only last from one to two years, and in a yard near by were a number waiting their turn, standing or lying in painful attitudes, one stretched out at length licking his poor legs. The men who drive these mules and stand knee-deep in this mud with naked legs also become affected and shorten their lives, but the unusual price of fifty cents per day secures men enough; and so cheap is this way of working that, rude as it is, it is doubtful whether mines so worked are not more profitable than those where the latest machinery is used, so terribly expensive is fuel and so scarce is water.

On the way back I saw a picture: through an opening of a fence of organ cactus, against a background of gray *adobé*, was leaning a tall, swarthy Mexican with wide *sombrero* and red *scrapé.* His *burro*, laden with panniers, stood with its bridle thrown over the branch of an oleander profuse in red blossoms, and overhead a bit of the bluest sky.

*February* 19*th.*—Woke at Querétaro, a fair city of say thirty thousand population, lying in the midst of the great plain, with water all about, and so is green and beautiful and fertile. It is the first city we have seen on a level site, and stands pleasantly in the midst of many umbrageous ash-trees, above which rise numerous domes and towers and steeples, hung with many bells; so that the hill a mile away is called Cerro de las Campanas, or "Hill of the Bells." Went to the plaza, a pretty, green spot, with abundant water brought five miles by an aqueduct, a gift from the Marquis de la Villar de la Aguilar. Bought some pottery in the market near by—two bottles and a vase —for twenty-eight cents. Rode out to the Cerro de las Campanas, from the highest point of which is a fair view of town and country smiling below. Here on the slope of the little hill looking toward the town, on the 19th of June, 1867, having been led thither from the Convent of the Capuchinas, by the way we came, Emperor Maximilian and the traitors Generals Miramon and Meji awere placed against a bit of low *adobé* wall used as a breastwork during the siege, and shot by sentence of a court-martial approved by General Escobedo and confirmed by Juarez. Goodly is the scene on which the emperor looked for the last time, if his heart were not too full of thoughts of his mother far away, when he asked as a last request that the ragged, sandalled patriots before him might be instructed not to disfigure his face with their bullets, so that she might see it once more. It is said that he was at first placed in the middle, but saying to General Miramon that the place of honor is for the bravest, gently led him there. Unfortunate Maximilian! Victim of the treachery of a Bonaparte, a race never sparing friend or foe! Stern, just, and wise Juarez, the truest friend thy country ever had, whom she may soon need again!

Yesterday at Irapuato, nineteen miles from Silao, fresh strawberries were brought, and it is said to be the only place where they can be had now. They are a long, pointed berry, looking unripe, but really quite sweet and relishable. At Marquez we were at the highest point on the road, 8134 feet above the sea, or 1849 feet higher than Mount Washington; the road descends again, then rises, then goes down into the basin some six hundred feet, where Mexico lies, about seventy-five hundred feet above the sea.

Another picture at Querétaro to-day. In the well-shaded plaza, on a spot of vividly green grass, the sun, glinting through the branches, falls in flecks on a soldier in white, relieved only by the black scabbard of the straight sword depending from his thigh, and his blue *scrapé* flung across his shoulder, standing like a statue, a thin wreath of smoke from his cigarette slowly rising and almost blending with the mist from a fountain behind him. Blooming shrubs all about. No stir in the air nor in anything save the mist of the fountain and the curling smoke.

## CHAPTER VII.

*We reach the Mexico Station of the Central Railroad—Iturbide Hotel—Paseo de la Reforma—The Alameda, or principal park—A brilliant equestrian picture—The National Theatre and Sarah Bernhardt.*

*February 20th, Sunday.*—Woke in the Mexico Station of the Central Railroad, twelve hundred and twenty-four miles from El Paso, where we entered the republic. The stars faded quickly from the east; soon the whole sky was filled with a light so dimmed with haze and dust that the peaks of the porphyritic mountains of the rim of the valley were scarcely visible, and far Ixtaccihuatl showed faintly and disappointingly. Conveyed by tramway to Iturbide Hotel, said most truly of all the stories about it, I should judge, to have been built by a wealthy Spaniard and rented for some time to the Emperor Iturbide, whence its name. It is a four-story building built of gray stone, tougher than what we have seen before, or perhaps igneous in origin, from the dead volcanoes hereabout, around a paved court, as all large houses are here, with floors, stairways and all, of solid stone or brick. The various parts we are used to seeing snugly placed in easy relations with one another are here scattered about in a rambling and disjointed way. There are *valets-de-chambre* in place of chambermaids, and although there are electric bells—and really the response is prompt enough—one wonders how it happens to be so and doesn't believe it likely to happen again.

We are well placed in a huge apartment giving on Sacramento Street by a balcony on the second story, where we can sit and see the life below. Here for the first time since we left New Orleans we leave our train for a hotel, and are to take our meals at the Café Anglais, near by the Iturbide, on the European plan, the table of the hotel not being thought well of. The cooking is a mixture of degenerate French and dirty Spanish, and we have *table d'hôte* of a dreary enough kind. Engaged, at the recommendation of Signor Rivaroll, a Mr. Benfield for guide and interpreter while here, at three dollars per day. He is a decayed English gentleman of say sixty-five, who has lived here since boyhood and seems mildly fit to show us the town.

This is a carnival day, and in the afternoon with Betty walked up our street and had seats for an hour by the Paseo de la Reforma, the fashionable drive, two miles long, extending in a straight line from the little circular plaza or *glorietta*, where is an equestrian statue of Charles IV., to the gates of Chapultepec, whose walls of white stone show fair on the isolated crag where it stands. The Paseo is more than a hundred feet wide, well paved, planted on each side with double rows of trees, under which are footways and massive seats of dull red stone. Within the distance of the first mile are imposing statues of Charles IV., Columbus, and Guatimozin, each in its *glorietta*, and within this extent every afternoon, between four and six o'clock, all the fashion of the city takes its exercise on horseback or in carriages, turning and going round and round over the same ground, the equestrians keeping the middle.

Lying along one side of this beautiful drive is the principal park or *Alameda*, as large pleasure-grounds or even public gardens are called throughout Mexico, because this one was originally planted with *alamos* or poplars. This spot was set apart by the city government in 1592 "for the ennoblement of Mexico and the recreation of its citizens." It includes a space about fifteen hundred feet long by seven hundred wide, and is charming, with its great trees, flowering shrubs, roses, and many fountains. The scene on the Paseo was quite animated, the carriages mostly ugly, heavy, and ill-hung hackney-coaches, with mules or only fairish horses to pull them, with now and then a better equipage, and sometimes a footman and coachman in livery ; but, on the whole, the cortege of carriages would make a sorry show in Central Park. The occupants mostly looked in the transition state, and unaccustomed to the provincialized Parisian raiment they had put on in place of the Mexican. With the body of the equestrians, however, it is quite different. The Mexican cavalier is, perhaps, as picturesque a figure as now remains in any land. These rode by in hundreds, sitting their horses admirably, wearing a richly ornamented *sombrero*, a tight jacket with close rows of little silver buttons, trousers of leather or heavy cloth, with two rows of broad, round spangles from the thigh down the outside of the leg to the bottom, buff leather boots equipped with heavy spurs of gold or silver—and such saddles ! all heavy, large, high-pommelled, embossed leather, abundant silver mountings, broad girths and ample housings. In some cases a handsome, neatly coiled lariat was hung behind the seat, and sometimes a sword at the pommel.

The Mexican rides with so cruel a bit that only the gentlest touch is needed, and a variegated cord of twisted silk or *maguey* fibre is quite enough to control his horse. Here and there a handsome señorita, with glorious eyes and black hair, rode by, usually with father and mother, or sister and brother, or other members of her family, for no respectable girl is allowed to be abroad without relative or duenna in company. The method of saluting acquaintances is peculiar. A gentleman, for instance, seeing a lady of his acquaintance in a balcony, makes an impressive gesture by quickly lifting his right hand and moving the two forefingers as if to inform her pointedly that he recognizes and salutes her. She in return—if she choose to do so, of course — makes a similar gesture in reply, when the cavalier takes off his *sombrero* by grasping the top of the crown and makes a sweeping salute with it. I saw such salutation between a pretty girl in a private carriage, with only a dumpy woman on the further side, appearing to be, from her inferior dress, an attendant or duenna. The salutation over, the cavalier, a dashing young blade, spurred his horse close beside the carriage, placed his nearer hand on its top, and with perfect ease kept his position until cavalier and equipage were out of sight—the bright, expressive eyes and smiling mouth of his inamorata testifying that his boldness was not displeasing.

In the evening went to the National Theatre

and saw Sarah Bernhardt as Theodora. The house is of solid stone, almost no wood used in it. It is nearly as large as the New York Academy of Music, and the auditorium is arranged in four circles of boxes, besides the usual parquet, which is fully respectable, and where seats are as high in price as in the boxes. The attendance was not large nor very enthusiastic, although the play would seem likely to rouse this people. The men have a habit of keeping their hats on before the play begins and between the acts, and of rising to face the spectators and stare at the ladies at leisure. The price of a ticket to the parquet for Bernhardt was four dollars. Her manager told me that she took three million francs in South America in three months. The dropcurtain is covered with advertising spaces painted in colors, and about two feet square, with some double that size, and three or four blanks. The effect was cheap and belittling to a degree. The performance began at a quarter to nine, the time set being half-past eight.

## CHAPTER VIII.

*We visit a private museum, also Chapultepec and the Monte de Piedad, or National Pawn-shop—The Cathedral—Its grandeur and impressiveness—An inspection of the National Museum and Academy of Fine Arts—The College of Medicine—The streets and houses of Mexico—How tortilla, the national corn food, is made.*

*February* 21*st.*—The morning cool and fresh and beautiful. No fire in the hotel, save in the kitchen, nor any way of having one, nor in any house in the city, I am told, and scarcely a chimney. Went by tramway to the end of the line, thence by a flatboat on the canal of Chalco, which runs alongside the Paseo de la Viga. This boat had cushioned seats along the sides and a low deal roof. The boatman propelled it by a pole, having only the runway of the slanting prow. The canal is, where we were on it, about sixty feet wide, the water foul, but not so bad as I expected from what I had read of it, and runs with considerable current. We went in this way to the first bridge, say three-quarters of a mile from the terminus of the tramway, landed on the opposite bank, and visited a sort of museum made in his private residence on the canal by a Spaniard—Juan Corano, a retired bull-fighter, who married a rich widow—where we saw many interesting things, such as arms, furniture, ornaments, etc., characteristically Mexican, and each good of its kind. The collection extends all through his private rooms, and is shown willingly, and even cordially, to callers. Nothing is for sale, and the half dollar I offered the young person who showed us about was positively declined. This beautiful and tasteful collection is well worth visiting. The charge made by the Indian who poled us up and back was fifty cents for a party of seven.

In the afternoon took a carriage and rode along the Paseo de la Reforma to Chapultepec, three miles from the hotel in a south-west direction, the old aqueduct bringing water to the city from the giant spring at Chapultepec over arches, being near at hand the greater part of the way. The intermediate country is perfectly level, as is the entire basin of Mexico, forty-five by thirty miles in extent. Chapultepec stands on the top of a steep, isolated, circular hill of porphyritic rock, say three hundred feet high. Montezuma is said to have had his palace here, and the Spaniards built a fortress on the site, and as it was surrounded by a marsh in earlier times it had great natural strength. The Government is fitting it up as a residence for the President, and by permission of the Governor of the National Palace, as the great building on the Cathedral plaza is called where all the officers of the Government are housed, we visited all the apartments, or nearly all, occupied by President Diaz and his family, now absent. He also has a house in town. These rooms were not long ago fitted up in a superb manner by a New York firm. The character of a fortress is disappearing.

The military academy is still here, but architects and workmen are changing the huge pile of buildings into a noble residence. Magnificent views are had from its marble terraces in every direction, partly obscured to us by the dust lifted by an unusual wind. I expected good views of Popocatapetl and Ixtaccihuatl— the former 17,782 feet, the latter 16,000 feet above the sea-level. These are peaks of the great Cordilleras range, are forty miles distant, and to-day hid in clouds. There has been no rain since last October in the valley, and the soil everywhere is parched, and deep with a light dust easily stirred by the wind, so that the city is partly veiled by it. In this neighborhood General Scott fought several battles in his flank movement on the city in 1847, forcing his way round from the east by the south to the west of Chapultepec, which was finally taken and the city was at his mercy. There was no carriage-way up the mountain then, I am told, but now one winds easily round it in a picturesque way among the enormous cypresses festooned with Spanish moss. While at the castle such dark and threatening clouds were massed by the wind as would surely have led to rain at home, and there were a few drops on the window-pane, but it passed away. Once in a great while, I am told, there comes a shower in the dry season, but the rule is no rain from the middle of June to October.

Visited the Monte de Piedad, or National Pawn-shop, one of the most interesting of the institutions of the city. It was founded in 1775 by a certain Pedro Romero de Terreros, owner of the famous mines of Real del Monte, for the kindly purpose of enabling the poor people of the city to obtain loans on personal property at the lowest possible rate of interest, he being moved thereto by the crying extortion practised by private pawnbrokers. To this end he endowed the establishment with three hundred thousand dollars, and it has since flourished, at first charging no interest whatever on its loans, and later just enough to pay expenses. Its average annual loans on pledges are said to be about one million dollars to from forty thousand to fifty thousand borrowers. A value is put to articles offered, by official appraisers, and they are then exposed for sale, at prices plainly stated on a card attached to each. Such as remain unsold at the end of a month are reduced in price and again exposed, to be still further marked down at the end of another month, and so on, reducing the price each month for six months, after which time they are sold at the best prices they will bring. If such prices will not repay the loan with the moderate interest exacted, the appraisers must personally make good the deficiency. Meantime, once a month, all such articles are offered at public auction, the upset price being the price on the ticket when the article is so offered. It occupies a handsome and commodious structure fronting the western façade of the Cathedral, erected for its use on the site formerly occupied by the palace of Cortez, and much of rich, quaint, and curious is to be seen in its show-cases and store-rooms.

Thence into the Cathedral, the " Holy Metropolitan Church of Mexico," and was much impressed by its size, vast spaces, and the richness of certain parts. It is said to stand on the site of the great Aztec temple. The first stone of the existing Cathedral was laid in 1573, the final dedication took place in 1667, the whole costing about two million dollars. The great bell, nineteen feet high, in the western tower was hung in 1792. It is four hundred and twenty-six feet in length by about two hundred wide, with an interior height of one hundred and eighty feet, and two towers of two hundred feet. The material of the walls is a gray stone harmonizing well with the basso-relievos, statues, friezes, bases, and capitals of white marble. The cornices are surrounded by balustrades of carved stone, on which stand stone vases and colossal stone statues of the doctors of the Church and other early dignitaries. Under the clock are blazoned the arms of the republic, a recent symbol of the supremacy of the State. The simple interior is in the Doric style; the central arches form a Latin cross, above which rises the dome with its paintings of sacred scenes, surmounted by its graceful lantern. The aisles are divided from the nave by twenty fluted columns supporting the vaulted roof. Outside the aisles are seven chapels on each side, each dedicated to some saint, with its altars, images, and pictures. Ranged in line down between the central rows of columns are two great altars rising almost to the roof—the Altar of Pardon, rich in gold and carving, and the main altar, approached by seven steps and supported by marble columns resembling malachite. But richer than these, massive, gorgeous, and deeply impressive, is the one rising at the north end from the pavement to the roof, called the Altar of Los Reyes—the Kings—all carved and gilded in a peculiarly rich and ornate style, first used, it is said, by the Spanish architect and sculptor Churriguara, whence it takes its name, Churriguaresque. It was executed by the artist who carved the Altar of Los Reyes in the Cathedral of Seville. Under it is buried the head of Hidalgo, brought from Guanajuato with honor. The choir occupies the space between the third and fourth rows of columns of the nave, midway between the Altar of Pardon and the Grand Altar, and while beautiful of itself, encumbers the middle space so as to mar the general effect. It is enclosed in front by a handsome railing of *tumbago*, a composite metal of gold, silver, and copper—worth more than its weight in silver—made in Macao, China. Rich and beautiful are the carvings of the brown oaken stalls, above which rise on either side for more than fifty feet the quaint and carven cases of two organs. In the central space, on high slanting desks, rest the huge choir-books of vellum, painted in black letters, dating from 1620. The wide passage from the choir to the Grand Altar is bordered by a massive railing of *tumbago*, as is the pedestal of the altar.

Thence to the National Museum, and were much interested, especially in the so-called Aztec remains. This is said to be the most complete collection of Aztec remains in existence. From what is shown here I certainly do not get any such impression of the civilization and greatness of that race as the glowing pages of Prescott prepared me for. Excepting the calendar stone, the sacrificial stone, and the great stone idol " Huitzilopochtli," all carved in a black, hard stone, and seeming, from their unlikeness to anything else here, to belong among the remains of another race, there is nothing in the collection, I should say, differing in kind or skill from what is shown in any fair collection of Indian relics. I do not pretend to be competent to judge, but venture the humble opinion that the accounts of the Aztecs at the time of the Spanish conquest, to which we are accustomed, are mostly fabrications, and that the Indians of that time were pretty much as I see them now in the parts we have visited, with the same simple habits, arts, manufactures, and characteristics. A great deal can be said on this point, but not by me.

Thence to the National Academy of Fine Arts, usually called the Academy of San Carlos. There are many pictures in suitable rooms, but nothing interested me much except the pictures by several pupils of the school and two by Felix Parra, formerly student and now professor in the same school, his "Las Casas" and "Galileo." My guide, Mr. Benfield, introduced me to a director of the school, Signor Lascurian, an agreeable and cultivated gentleman, who speaks English well, and who will make me known to Professor Parra.

Passed the entire afternoon with guide going to junk-shops, pawnbroker-shops, and queer, out-of-the-way places. The junk-shops are booths on the squares, and display a queer lot of "auld nick nackets"—savage knives, the queerest old locks, etc. Many of these booths are ranged along the west side of the plaza by the beautiful Church of Santo Domingo. Hard by is the massive building—now occupied by the College of Medicine—built for the use of the Inquisition, which noble and civilizing institution was set agoing at once after the conquest and held its first *auto da fé* in 1574, when "twenty-one pestilent Lutherans" were burned. Its last years were spent in fighting liberalism, and its last victim the patriot Morelos, who was put to death as a "traitor to God, to the King, and to the Pope," on the 26th of November, 1815.

The streets of Mexico are not at all so picturesque as those of the smaller cities, this quality having been considerably modernized away. The houses, mostly of one story, present rather a mean appearance seen from the front; even the large, fine ones—and there are many of these—hiding their splendor behind plain walls and barred windows, not in a fashionable quarter by themselves, but mixed in with the residences of the poor. It is the custom to let the front rooms of the first floor for business purposes; and the city residence of the rich family of the Escandrons, perhaps the finest house in Mexico, has over the windows of one side of the wide entrance in big letters the sign of the newspaper *Mexican Financier*. The living-rooms of the good houses are on the second story, and when the windows are thrown open and the balconies, showy with many colored awnings, are filled with family groups, the scene is cheerful enough, and is heightened by the lively colors used in painting the exteriors. But quaintness and mellow richness of form and color is given by the numerous old churches and other ecclesiastical establishments which rise on every hand, vast, and compelling the attention at all times.

Passing along one of the sides of the huge National Palace I looked into an, or rather *the* engine-house of the city quartered in a gloomy room on the ground floor. There was a steamer, said not to be in order, and two of the oddest old hand-engines extant. This is the preparation of the city against fires, but why should they make any? The houses are all stone and have no chimneys nor fires except a charcoal range or brazier standing on a stone floor, and generally in the open air in the courts.

Adjoining the engine-house are some little shops where the *tortilla*, the national corn food, is made and served hot from the fire. The *tortilla* is the main article of food among the native Indians all over Mexico, and is presumably made as at the time of the conquest. The women of each family prepare these little cakes daily, and the labor of doing it is so great as to absorb almost all their time. They are made by soaking the kernels of Indian corn in a weak lye until the hull is easily removed, and macerating the grains on a hollow stone called *metate*, kept for the purpose, then flattening the pulp in the palms of the hands into small, thin, round cakes, which are cooked over a charcoal fire much as we do our buckwheat-cakes. They are eaten plain or with a little hashed meat and vegetables, red pepper predominating, folded in like the old-fashioned New England turnover and fried in fat. These with several coarse varieties of stewed beans, called *frijole*, constitute almost the entire food of the great bulk of the population. "Take away his *tortilla*," said Signor Rivaroll, chief interpreter of our party, "and you would reduce the Mexican to despair. Nothing could possibly take its place."

Beef is fairly good in the City of Mexico, and is conveyed from the slaughter-houses to the shops in quarters, suspended by hooks on huge frames fitted to the backs of stout mules. Poultry is good and cheap, and vegetables abundant, so that there is little excuse for the poor living here.

Made some purchases. The Mexican shopkeeper is a consummate rascal in his dealings. He lies in the most unblushing manner, and begins by asking three or four times the price he is content to take. The most honest dealers are the foreigners in trade here, English, Germans, and Americans. There are good stores of jewelry, etc., only fair of dry-goods. The shops are all small, and the bulk of the customers poor. There is no observance of the courtesy of the sidewalk, no keeping of the right hand in walking. Everybody moves straight on and only deflects when obliged to. This gives the body of promenaders a bumpkin appearance, like the walks of a country town on circus day. The public facilities for getting about are excellent. Lines of tramway diverge in all directions from the Cathedral plaza, and the service is cheap and good. The city is admirably policed both by a mounted force and patrolmen, the latter carrying lanterns at night, which they set down from time to time in the middle of the streets. These are well lighted, the more important ones by the electric light.

In the evening went to Orrin's Circus, a permanent establishment here, and saw a performance for the benefit of a hospital for Americans taken sick in the city. Our Minister, Mr. Manning, laid the corner-stone of the hospital to-day, Washington's birthday, kept as a national holiday in Mexico.

## CHAPTER IX.

*Go to Guadalupe by tramcar—A disappointment—Legend of Our Lady of Guadalupe—The sacred spring—" The Chapel of the Well" and " The Chapel of the Little Hill"—A description of the city and of the enormous ditch Tajo de Nochistongo.*

*February* 23*d.*—In the morning went to Guadalupe, two and a half miles north of the city, by tramway. The tramcars are drawn always by mules, going at a gallop, lashed and objurgated all the way by swarthy conductors dressed in blue tunics, high boots, gray felt *sombreros*, wearing a brass horn slung over the shoulder, giving harsh notice of our dusty approach. Tried hard on the way to see Popocatapetl, but clouds hid it, although the air was fairly clear. I have been much disappointed about this mountain, not having had at all a fair view, and expecting it to be a prominent feature. Here where Guadalupe now stands, in 1531—so the legend is—on the morning of the 9th of December, Juan Diego, a poor native Indian, was on his way to mass, when he heard angelic music and the voice of a Lady, who, out of gleaming splendors, bade him go to the bishop and say it was her will that he build a temple on that spot. He obeyed, but the bishop refused to believe the prodigy. He returned to the Lady, who heard his report and bade him come to her again; and when he did so on the following Sunday she ordered him again to go and again command the bishop to build the temple, who was still incredulous. The Indian then sought the Lady and asked that he might have some sure sign of her appearance to take back, and was told to come next day, when she gave him a miraculous flower and bade him carry it to the bishop. He wrapped this in his *tilma* or cloth tunic, and lo! when he unfolded it there was imprinted on the tunic in beautiful colors a perfect image of the Virgin; and from the spot where had stood most holy Mary gushed forth a spring of medicinal water, the antidote of all infirmities.

Of course the bishop was convinced, and built a church on the spot where the Virgin appeared, who, under the title of "Our Lady of Guadalupe," is the patron saint and most venerated name in Mexico. The miracle was confirmed by Rome, 1754, and the Virgin of Guadalupe was declared the patroness and protectress of New Spain. One of the first acts of the New Republic, 1824, was to decree the 12th of December a national holiday. She epitomizes the national life. Especially is she the divinity of the Indians, thousands of whom make long pilgrimages to her shrine on the 12th of December of each year.

The Church of Nuestra Señora de Guadalupe is rather modern, and is the fourth built for housing the miraculous image, and was completed in 1709. It has a frescoed dome one hundred and twenty-five feet high. This church, very rich in jewels, gold, and silver, has been *relieved* by the Government of nearly all its wealth, but has a massive silver railing enclosing the chancel and running from the altar to the choir. The miraculous picture of the Virgin hangs in a tabernacle in a frame of mingled gold and silver covered with plate glass, and is fairly drawn on coarse cloth and has good coloring. All who have the faith to believe it of miraculous origin so believe. "Without faith ye can do nothing."

The spring is an ample, mild, sulphur water with a not disagreeable taste, and the small copper pail dipping into it is in constant use; and such motley and wild throngs as flock to its sacred water to-day! The spring is in the anteroom of a little chapel called Capilla del Pocito, "The Chapel of the Well," having a charming dome of enamelled tiles. On the top of the hill is the Capilla del Cerrito, "The Chapel of the

Little Hill," marking the spot where Juan Diego cut the roses, reached by a wide stairway winding up the rock. Part way up the hill on the west side is a curious grotto made by excavating several rooms in the hillside and lining the wall with broken bits of all kinds of pottery, producing a pretty effect in mosaic, a work of infinite patience done by some toiler unknown to fame whose patchworks continue to praise him.

In the afternoon took carriage and shopped till dinner with wife, children, and guide. The city is laid out in wide streets running at right angles, but for the most part badly paved and poorly kept, as much so, I should say, as the greater parts of New York and Brooklyn. It stands in the lowest part of a plain of about thirty by forty miles, this plain being the bottom of a bowl whose rim is an almost unbroken circle of high mountains. This plain is seventy-five hundred feet above the sea, and so situated that, so far, it has not been possible to drain it. Consequently the city stands on the sewage of more than three hundred and fifty years, having been founded by Cortez in 1521. The population of the city proper is about three hundred thousand. In spite of the great advantage of its elevation, so that noxious emanations from the putrid soil are dissipated in the rarefied air,

Mexico, which should be one of the healthiest, is really one of the most unhealthy cities in the world. There can be no improvement until there is a system of drainage, and to this problem the best talent and wisdom of the republic is devoting itself. This whole basin was once a lake, then by evaporation a swamp, and now, from the same cause, firm, dry land, excepting about one tenth of its surface covered by four primeval lakes without outlet.

Texcoco, the only salt lake, is on the lowest level, and contains seventy-seven square miles, the great square of the capital being only two feet higher than its mean level. Ochimilco, with fifty square miles of surface, is three and a half feet higher than Texcoco, and Zumpango is twenty-nine feet higher than the city. Of course the danger of inundation is always imminent, the protection from it being only partial. There have been five of these inundations, the last one continuing from 1629 to 1634. On a street corner, at a height of from twelve to fifteen feet from the pavement, is affixed to a wall a grotesque head marking the highest point reached by the water in 1629.

In 1607 the Viceroy employed Enrico Martinez, a native of Germany, to devise a plan to protect the city. He proposed to make a tunnel through a notch of the mountains and carry off the surplus water of the lakes, and when afterward this was found to be too small, it was opened at the top and converted into a huge dike called *Tajo de Nochistongo*, an enormous ditch, said to be the most extensive earth-cutting in existence. Its length is 67,537 feet, its greatest depth 197 feet, and greatest breadth 361 feet. It was nearly two hundred years building, and is said to have cost the lives of seventy thousand natives. A handsome pedestal and bust stand in the Cathedral plaza erected to Martinez, and on one side is an index showing the rise and fall of the threatening water in the lakes.

But all that has been done hitherto is quite insufficient for the drainage of the city and the lakes. There is but one effectual way, and that a city like Chicago, for instance, would have put into use long ago. There must be cut sheer through the rim of the surrounding mountains such an outlet as will suffice to do the work, and then the City of Mexico will be a most delightful and healthy city. As it is, all forms of malaria sweep off the population to an alarming extent, and only the altitude of the city saves it from plagues rendering it uninhabitable.

I should have said that connected with the Chapel on the Hill is a cemetery with many fine tombs of a fashion strange to me, where lie the dead of leading families, among them Santa

Aña, who sought this spot as sanctified ground. In this village was signed the treaty of Guadalupe-Hidalgo between the United States and Mexico at the close of the war, February 2d, 1848.

## CHAPTER X.

*We attend mass at the Cathedral—The " Tree of the Dismal Night"— Toluca—Pulque and how it is made—Market-day in Toluca—The Nevado de Toluca Mountain—A grand view from the Castle of Chapultepec—Famous cypress-trees—A magnificent spring of water—Tacubaya and its Observatory.*

*February 24th.*—In the morning attended mass in the Cathedral. Greatly impressed by the services in the vast space, with the music and colors. At its close went into the sacristy, where the attendants were putting away the vestments into huge mahogany drawers with great brass handles and mountings. Brockelhurst, the English traveller, who has written an interesting book on Mexico, states that he was shown some vestments presented to the Cathedral by Isabella of Spain of great richness and weight. My guide, at my request, asked a padre who chanced to be in the sacristy for a sight of them. The father assured us in the most positive way that he had seen what Brockelhurst had written about them, and that it is pure fiction.

In the afternoon rode out to the *Arbol de la Noche Triste*, or "Tree of the Dismal Night," where Cortez, July 1st, 1521, being repulsed in his attack on the city and in great danger of the utter destruction of his small force, sat down and wept as his men in retreat filed by in the darkness of the night. It is a species of cypress —the same as the trees at Chapultepec—and is gnarled and knotted into huge knobs at the base of the trunk, with a few scanty, straggling branches and very little foliage—looking, indeed, as if it could not live a great many years longer. An attempt to burn it some few years ago was so nearly successful that an opening was made through it. It is now protected by a high iron railing, and also, it is said, by a special policeman, although I saw nothing of him. The place is called Popotla, and a few steps from the tree is the quaint and mouldering church of San Esteban.

We rode alongside the aqueduct which for a hundred years has brought from a famous spring at Chapultepec pure water into the city, and visited two fountains of carved stone, into whose great basins this water came for the public use. Called on Mr. Porch, our Consul-General here, and subscribed to the American hospital fund. Looked into the National Library housed in the beautiful church San

Augustin, containing two hundred thousand volumes, said to be valuable and well arranged, coming largely from the libraries of the suppressed religious orders. If so there must be much trash, I should say. Also to the cemetery connected with the Church of San Fernando, where is a fine tomb to Juarez, a Greek portico, and within, his effigy, the size of life, reclining its head in the lap of a weeping figure, representing, I suppose, the Republic—all done in Italian marble. A light shower wetting the pavement at 4 P.M. From our balcony saw a beautiful rainbow.

*February 25th.*—At 8 P.M. went by Mexican National Railroad across the westward range of mountains known as Las Cruces to Toluca, capital of the State of Mexico, situated in a great fertile plain forty-six miles from the city. At the highest point, Cima, we were 10,280 feet above the sea. Yet these heights were cultivated with the crops of the plains below, and the vegetation much the same, with grass—now dry —to the tops of the highest peaks. The views up and down are magnificent and beautiful, and the day memorable.

We dined at the Leon de Oro and returned in the afternoon. At dinner drank my first and only glass of *pulque*, the lager beer of Mexico. It is of the color of thin buttermilk and tastes something like it, with a small addition of rotten egg. It is made from the fermented juice of the *maguey* plant, and contains about the same amount of alcohol as lager beer, from five to seven per cent. The *maguey* or centuryplant, called also the American aloe, is grown largely hereabout, and still more largely in the districts to the east of the City of Mexico, set in vast plantations and cultivated with much care, watched carefully, and when about ten years old, having been kept from flowering in the mean time, just at the time of efflorescence, the central stalk is cut out so as to leave a cavity into which the abundant juice flows.

This is carefully gathered twice a day into sacks of sheep-skins and carried on the back of the universal donkey to the *tenacal* or fermenting-house on each plantation, mingled with a due proportion of rotten curd left over from a previous fermentation, poured on cow-hides with the hairy side up, made into vats by stretching them on frames, and after fermenting there about three hours is drawn into skin-sacks or barrels for shipment to the *pulquerias* or retail shops of the capital, to be drunk within the next twelve hours, after which it becomes sour and unfit for use. A *pulque* train comes in every morning from Apam, fifty miles east of the capital, and it is said the Government receives a thousand dollars a day in duty and the railroads a like sum in freight on the *pulque* coming into the city. It is retailed at about five cents a quart, is drunk almost universally, and foreigners are said to soon become fond of it and to find it a healthy beverage.

It was market-day in Toluca, and as many as a thousand Indians, I should say, were in the market square, forming one of the most characteristic gatherings of natives we have seen. The articles for sale were few and simple, hats of straw, *rebozos* of cotton, cheap pottery, etc., but the chaffering went on with all the earnestness and more gesticulation than on the New York Stock Exchange.

The plain of Toluca owes its greater fertility to the important stream of Rio Lerma. To the west rises the Nevado de Toluca, fifteen thousand feet above the sea-level, the fourth mountain in Mexico, its top shining with perpetual snow. It is an extinct volcano, and as we left the station to return the sun fell brightly on the heights and peaks of the outer rim of the old crater, so that they shone like the delectable mountains of Bunyan's Pilgrim.

The town has about ten thousand population, and although old has a more modern look than almost any one we have seen. A picture: a great plain stretching away on every side to meet purple mountains of fantastic forms, and westward, rising into the clouds, the shining top of the Nevado de Toluca. Many fields, with irrigating rivulets, and a long, narrow lake. Many gray stone churches lifting their yellow domes into the clear, warm air. Three native Mexicans, one in red, one in blue, one in white, trudging along a broad, dusty highway, each with a pannier on his back, and three *burros* similarly laden. Near at hand, in another wide highway intersecting the first, a drove of laden mules moving slowly, the muleteers, in many-colored *scrapés* and dusty sandals, following on foot.

The fertile land of the plain is owned by a few rich proprietors. In one field I counted seventeen ploughs going, drawn by as many yoke of oxen harnessed by the horns. These ploughs, too, seemed to be of Yankee make, but usually is only a stick which stirs the soil without turning it over. As we approached the mountains in returning, I saw clouds settled down below the highest peaks. These had lifted when we were at the summit, but had left snow visible for a mile or two and quite copious rain.

*February 26th.*—Drove out to Chapultepec by the Paseo de la Reforma. Went up to the paved platform of the second story of the castle and carefully looked from all points of the compass over the broad valley of Mexico. Grand mountains rise all about. The snowy heads of Popocatapetl and Ixtaccihuatl were hid in clouds. It is a grand and beautiful panorama. The city with its great number of domes and spires shone in the quivering, hazy light, three miles away. It does not occupy the ground one would expect a city of from two hundred and fifty to three hundred thousand to do. With more than a third of the population of Brooklyn, I should not think it covered more than a sixth as much ground, although its principal streets are wider and a large proportion of its houses not more than one story. To the west rises the extinct volcanic mountain Ajusco, which must have been famous in its day if, as our guide stated, its lava had flowed almost to the Pacific —nigh one hundred and twenty miles!

Rode and walked among the famous cypress-trees at the foot of the hill, said to have been of size in the days of Montezuma. Measured the largest and found it a few inches short of forty-one feet in circumference. I think it over one hundred and fifty feet high, and it appears to have had the upper part of its stem broken off. These avenues of hoary trees are said to be what is meant by the " Halls of the Montezumas." Saw pouring out of the ground at the base of the mound of Chapultepec the pure water of a magnificent spring, flowing now, it is thought, as when the Aztec kings ruled in this valley. It is now pumped by steam up to a height sufficient to pour it into the old open stone aqueduct which carries it into the heart of the city and to the fountains I saw yesterday. There is also a second aqueduct running back into the Las Cruces Mountains we crossed yesterday, and taking up one of its streams and delivering it into the city. The water of one is soft, of the other hard, and both good, pure water, I should think. Most of the better sort of houses in the city have water brought in by pipes. The families of the poorer sort buy it at a low rate from peddlers or supply themselves from the numerous fountains.

Drove from Chapultepec across to Tacubaya, a town of about eight thousand, said to be the handsomest in the valley, where are suburban residences with charming gardens, and sent our guide in to ask the director of the National Observatory about the Southern Cross. He stated it came to the meridian at 1.30 A.M., and could be well seen at midnight in the city. The Observatory is housed in the ex-palace of the archbishop. Indeed, the schools of science and art are pretty much all in old religious establishments, these haunts of bigotry and superstition being lit up and purged by the light of science, wherein is the presage of a better future for this land.

Lunched at Naylor's restaurant near the Cathedral. He had an English father, but was born here of a Spanish mother, and neither his look, manner, nor cuisine indicated his descent, although he specially cultivates Americans by promises of roast beef and mince-pies. There was a little sprinkle of rain this afternoon and clouds which looked capable of much, but they scattered as usual, rain in any quantity being among the rarest incidents now for three months to come.

I neglected to say that at the foot of the hill of Chapultepec stands a handsome column erected, as the inscription says, " To the Memory of the Cadets of the Military College who died as heroes die in the North American Invasion." These were mere lads who fell fighting obstinately, to the number of forty, in the defence of Chapultepec.

# CHAPTER XI.

*We visit the Methodist Church—Dine at the Concordia Restaurant—Witness a bull-fight—A description of the repulsive scenes there enacted.*

*February 27th, Sunday.*—Cloudy and cooler, but the thermometer in my room does not vary more than three degrees, ranging from sixty-four to sixty-seven. This is in a room facing north, with thick walls, and not much affected by the weather outside. Attended service in the Methodist Church, held by Bishop Hirst, of Buffalo, N. Y. The Methodists have bought an old convent and hold services in what was the chapel, a simple and severely handsome room. Took dinner at the Concordia Restaurant, the Delmonico of Mexico. My party consisted of six persons. Had tomato soup, fish with potatoes, chicken fricassee with mushrooms, roast beef with mashed potatoes, lettuce salad, ice cream, Roquefort cheese, coffee with fruit, the meal well cooked, in a cool, quaint room of the red-walled convent, now a restaurant. Not anywhere else in the city, from what I could learn, is a restaurant equal to so modest a *menu* as this.

Went in the afternoon to a bull-fight at the Arquitectos Ring, opened to the public last Sunday for the first time. For twenty years this national amusement has been prohibited within the city limits, but allowed again by the Congress at its last session. In consequence this Ring is now completed and opened. Another is being erected on the fashionable drive of the Reforma, and am informed five permits altogether have been granted for building these. This would seem to indicate a growing desire for this form of amusement; and in the *Two Republics* of this morning I find the following: " To-day is a red-letter day in the history of bull-fighting in Mexico, which will always be talked of by the numerous admirers of the sport. The great, only, and famous Mazzantini makes his *début* in Mexico." This is a famous *toreador* who has come from Spain to Puebla, where it is said he is to be paid fifteen thousand dollars for two performances. It is said that from four to five thousand people went from here to witness his performance to-day at Puebla.

To offset this attraction, the management of the Arquitectos Ring have obtained three Spanish *toreadors*, who, without the fame of the illustrious Mazzantini, are yet of sufficient renown to create a stir of expectation, and the red bill of the performance now before me promises six bulls *á muerte*, or done to death, all from the "pen of Guadalupe," one of these to be a *toro embolado*—that is, a bull who has had his horns sawed off and the stumps wrapped in flax so as to be harmless, in this condition to be set upon by all the vagabonds present who choose to enter the ring and tease him.

The Ring of Arquitectos is about one hundred and twenty feet in diameter, the hard earth enclosed being perfectly flat, smooth, and lightly sprinkled with sand. The barrier is about five and a half feet high, stoutly made of a frame of timber covered and faced with jointed boards planed and matched, making a perfect circle. Back of this is a second barrier, with a space of some six feet between. This is for greater safety in case the bull should leap over the first. Beginning immediately behind this second barrier rises a series of seats one above another, eight in all, and extending round the arena. Still above these is a tier of boxes extending round the circle with back and roof, but open in front and at the sides, each having comfortable chairs for eight. This ring is said to afford sitting and standing room for sixteen thousand people, and I estimate about twelve thousand were present to-day.

At equal distances apart are six retreats for

the performers, consisting of a square shield of jointed boards like the barrier—say five feet each way—set out from the barrier two feet, so that when too hardly pressed a man can step in behind it and be out of the bull's reach. At one point the barrier is pierced for two stout gates opening inward to admit the bull, living, into the arena, and permit him to be dragged out when dead. About twenty feet to one side of this is a similar opening and gates for the passage of the performers—men and horses. Directly opposite this last is the box, distinguished by some decorations of gaudy strips of cotton, where the judges sit. In the rear of the boxes, at frequent intervals, are staves from which colored flags float, and two military bands play alternately, stationed on the lower seats, equidistant from the judges' box and the gates.

As the time approached the vast crowd manifested its eagerness by wild cries, stamping of the feet, and that indescribable bass hum which easily deepens into a roar and strikes one with a sort of awe. Precisely at four o'clock the doors opposite the judges' box were thrown open, and in rich dresses, mostly like those shown on the stage as the court costumes of three hundred years ago, came the performers in the following order: First, the three *espadas*, as they are called on the bill, being the same as *matadors*, marching abreast, each carrying in his right hand a long, slender rapier with which he puts the bull to death, in his left a red flag, or rather, from its shape, a sort of mantle. Next, the *banderilleros*, three in number, carrying darts with shafts gaily decked with knots of ribbon, also bright mantles like the others; then several *chulos* and *capas* with bright-colored cloths. Behind these, the *picadors* on horseback, three of these, bearing long pikes with a pointed iron two inches long set into the end. Last came three gaily-harnessed mules abreast, with painted whiffle-trees held up and carried by an attendant in livery.

This procession moved directly across the arena to the stand of the judges, whom they saluted by doffing their hats and a low obeisance, then quickly scattered themselves over the arena, apparently in a disorderly way, but doubtless in regulation positions; and the other doors opening at once, a black bull appeared, weighing, I should say, not more than twelve hundred pounds, looking civil enough, and as if he would like nothing so well as to be let alone. He had evidently been operated on to rouse him to a show of fierceness, for a slight stain of blood showed below a great rosette on one shoulder, held there, as could easily be guessed, by a dart firmly stuck into the flesh.

As he came into the arena he looked quietly round in a sort of wonder on the vast crowd applauding his sturdy appearance, which promised sport, and would in all likelihood have done nothing whatever but walk back to his pen had not a *picador* rode close before him, when he lowered his horns, and in a slow, deliberate way charged the *picador*, who, partly wheeling, thrust his pike into the bull's shoulder and sought to bear him back. But the momentum of the bull was too great, and the *picador's* horse, a wretched hack, was forced close up to the barrier and fell heavily, his rider tumbling in a heap on the further side from the bull, who immediately fell back of his own accord, being at once roused again, by shaking red cloths before him, to chase the *banderilleros* about in a lumbering way. These easily avoided him by stepping nimbly to one side, or in some cases dodging behind the wooden shields.

Again a *picador* crossed the bull's way and was charged on as before, but by thrusting the point of his pike into the bull's shoulder and firmly pressing on it, while at the same time he moved his horse obliquely forward, he got no harm. The first horse struck by the bull was got up, led out, and, as I was informed, shot, having been gored by the bull's horns. The horses are covered by their trappings, especially by a thick leathern shield covering the entire hind half of the body, which it not only protects from the bull's horns, but so hides him that little more than the legs can be seen.

By this time a quarter of an hour had passed since the baiting began ; the bull's eyes were bloodshot, little streams of blood came from the wounds in his shoulders, and he breathed heavily. Then a *banderillero* came before him with a dart in each hand, and hurling them both at once by a dexterous movement, infixed them in each shoulder and stepped lightly aside. This was really cleverly done and called out a roar of applause. This was repeated after a few seconds, but the tortured animal was not to be goaded into further demonstrations.

Then stepped to the front the " Primer Espada José Machio," from the great amphitheatres of Spain. He wore a tight-fitting suit of rich goods in several colors, is a tall, fine figure of a man, and had his hair curiously done up in a club or great knot on the top of his head. He held a long, slender rapier in his right hand, in his left a red cloth, one side of which is fastened to a rod so that it is kept displayed. He bowed to the judges and to the spectators, who received him with such a greeting as is given to an actor of fame making his *début*. He moved slowly toward the bull, taking a position so that the latter would pass near him when he should be roused by the *capas*, who sought to lead him on by spreading out their red mantles on the ground before him, and when at last the bull stepped forward the *matador* thrust at him, but failed to hit him.

A hiss went up from parts of the crowd, for it is the proper thing to kill at the first stroke. The *matador* bowed with a deprecating gesture, as much as to say, " Be a little patient, good people, and you shall see something yet worthy the great José Machio." Then a second chance offering, with a movement so quick as hardly to attract attention he thrust the long blade of his rapier obliquely backward and downward to its entire length, from a point between the shoulder-blades, leaving it in the wound. The bull reeled for an instant, fell on his knees, slowly turned his head with a piteous look at the howling mob around him, rose again to his feet, took half a dozen steps, and fell prone on his side. An attendant stepped forward, thrust a dagger into a vertebra of the neck, the harnessed mules came gaily in, and with a blare of wild music from the band he was dragged by the neck out at the door he had entered twenty minutes before. I left my box at once and betook myself to the street before the next bull was brought in, but before I had got out of hearing a long, hoarse roar rose over the advent of a new victim.

To me, who love most animals, who recognize in them in a less degree the emotions and many of the mental traits, and certainly a great share of the susceptibility to pain of the human race, the spectacle I had just witnessed was inexpressibly shocking. That thousands of men, women, and children should gather to see a poor animal tortured to death, that such spectacles of barbarity should constitute a national amusement, of which all classes are said to be passionately fond, gives me a baser idea of human nature than has ever presented itself to me before. I cannot imagine a nation progressing in civilization and greatness with a principal amusement so savage and degrading.

The people filling the seats of the amphitheatre seemed to be of the average class of citizens; indeed, there were not many national costumes to be seen—more Derby hats than *sombreros*. To be sure there were at least ten men to one woman, but I saw many boxes occupied by what a gentleman well acquainted in the city assured me are quite respectable families, father, mother, children, as we see in the theatres at home. No countries except Spanish countries have this amusement; no nations are so cruel. This horrid and disgusting sport seems natural to the Spanish portion of this people.

On the way to the hotel stopped at the Tivoli Gardens, a fashionable resort where refreshments are served in little arbors, and had with one of our interpreters a bottle of German beer for one dollar and twenty-five cents, which would cost perhaps forty cents in New York.

## CHAPTER XII.

*A "Norther" and its result—A ride to Apizaco—
We see a pretty bit of scenery—San Juan Teotihuacan and its two ancient pyramids—A brilliant view of Ixtaccihuatl and Popocatapetl—
Puebla and what we saw there.*

*February 28th.*—There is what is called a
" Norther" prevailing this morning, and my
thermometer shows a fall of ten degrees, showing fifty-six degrees; but I am informed that out
of doors it shows forty-seven degrees. At home
I should certainly need a fire, and have got out
my heavy overcoat. All the guests are com-
plaining of the cold, but there is not a fire in
the great hotel or the facilities for one. I said
to one of our interpreters that it seemed to
me that comfortable citizens here, used to warm
weather, must feel such a turn of chill, and
would find a fire in their sitting-rooms quite
necessary. His answer was that the people re-
tire so late and rise so late as to escape a cold
morning.

Betty showing signs of illness, I sent for Dr.
Parsons, two years ago from Cambridge, near
Boston, and now at the head of the American

hospital here, who calls it intermittent fever, and is giving two grains of quinine each two hours.

Mr. R. B. Lawrence, of Medford, Mass., one of our party, Secretary of the Appalachian Club, left here on Saturday by the Morelos Railroad for Amecameca, six miles from the base of Popocatapetl, whence he rode fifteen miles on horseback to the " Ranch," twelve thousand feet above the sea, passed the night there, and Sunday morning, with a party of guides, attempted to reach the top. He found the heavy snowfall of the day before had obliterated all traces of the paths and was obliged to return.

*March 1st.*—Betty had high fever all night. Arranged for copy of his "Galileo" with Professor Felix Parra. Dr. Parsons decided Betty might go to Puebla with the party, and I arranged with him to go with us. We brought her down-stairs, being quite weak, but fever gone. Went to station of Vera Cruz Railroad in doctor's carriage, and put her directly to bed in section seven of Pullman sleeper Holden. Her fever did not return. Rode on Vera Cruz Railroad—capital road—to Apizaco, passing through San Juan Teotihuacan, where we saw the pyramids near at hand, Apam, the centre of the *pulque* district, etc.

At Apizaco our train went on a branch road to Puebla, one hundred and sixteen miles from Mexico, reaching it at 8.30 P.M., having left Mexico at 3 P.M. The road runs over a level plain, well cultivated, with all aspects of nature and man strange and picturesque and steeped in colors of romance. Wide plains, parched and dusty, low, white villages with church-spires rising in the pure air, and all around such mountains with such tints on them as one only sees in pictures of the imagination done with pen or pencil.

At San Juan Teotihuacan, twenty-seven miles from the city, are two ancient pyramids, so called, said to have been erected by the Toltecs in honor of the sun and moon respectively. The larger—to the sun—is one hundred and eighty feet high and six hundred and eighty-two feet long at the base. These are plainly visible from the road, and as we are carefully to see the fully more interesting one at Cholula, no stop is made here.

As we drew near Apam, lo! a spectacle memorable and magnificent beyond words! The sun was nigh his set in a glory of color, when the clouds, which whenever I have tried to see them obscured and hid the august forms of Ixtaccihuatl and Popocatapetl, parted and vanished, and nearest the west, where the splendor was greatest, lay, as on a gigantic bier, the figure of the " White Woman," her head toward the sunset, her pulseless bosom cold and glistening in eternal snow, and at her feet Popocatapetl, like a gigantic mourner, towering far above all confusion of colors and tints and accidents of earth into the blue serene, hooded and draped in immaculate white. Across the plain to the east of the road rose snow-crowned the shapely crag of Malinche, the seventh mountain in height of Mexico.

*March 2d.*—Woke at Puebla. Betty had a good night and is free from fever this morning. The sun rose in a cloudless sky, and both Popocatapetl and Ixtaccihuatl stood out clear and free of clouds from base to summit on one hand and on the other Malinche. Puebla is an important city, and, in the Mexican sense, prosperous. It is the capital of the State of the same name and contains seventy thousand population, contesting with Leon the honor of being the second city in the republic.

The Cathedral is large and fine, but I found the Church of San Francisco more to my mind and almost more interesting than any church I have seen. In the lavatory is a beautiful laver of tile work, three bowls set in an oblong case of colored tiles, themselves also made from tiles, with a fountain above to supply them, also in tiles—all so charming I could have carried it off bodily. Above hung a prayer in Latin, to the effect that God would grant clean hands and strong, with a pure heart, to do His work and will. The altar is a beautiful one.

In the tabernacle is kept the image of Nuestra Señora de los Remedios, also called La Conquestadora, a little figure carved in wood, say eight inches tall, with a tiny baby on its arm, said to have been presented by Cortez to an Indian ally. It is said that the identity of the image is shown by documents. The wooden stalls in the choir are finely carved, and such a quaint old organ! There are warm sulphur baths here amply supplied from a big spring of tepid water.

In the evening went to the School of Meteorology, located, as most institutions of learning are, in a secularized convent, to see the Southern Cross. Went up on the brick roof by the light of a lantern and remained three hours, but clouds hindered. There was a moon, and the long stretches of flat roofs swelling into domes and various convexities to conform to the arched ceilings below—the space included originally in the convent walls was not less than a Brooklyn block—the dusty courts below with fountains and trees, the tall Cathedral towers, the sky mottled with broken masses of clouds, the constant clangor of bells all over the city, made an impressive scene. More than half of the space of this city was occupied by the various ecclesiastic establishments, many of enormous size.

## CHAPTER XIII.

*A ride to Cholula and something about it and its pyramid—The Franciscan Monastery—Pleasant cogitations—We set off for Tlascala and visit its Governor—The old Church of San Francisco—The descent to the Tierras Calientes—We linger at Orizaba and enjoy its many beauties—Start for Mexico City—A fine view of the Southern Cross.*

*March 3d.*—In the morning went by tramway to Cholula. Exceedingly interesting ride of eight miles across the charming valley of the Atoyac. The broad fields more fertile by reason of more water; everywhere in sight objects of artistic and poetic interest; gray arches of aqueducts and bridges; towers and crosses of old, worn stone; churches with colored façades and domes; all around clear-cut, multiform mountains; and central figure in the landscape the Church of Nuestra de los Remédios towering from the pyramid of Cholula, on the razed top of which it stands two hundred and four feet above the level plain.

The general form of the mound is pyramidal, but through the changes made by the hand of time and man and the confusion of outline wrought by a quite heavy growth of trees and bushes all up and down its sides, I could myself see few marks of an artificial structure. The Spaniards cut the top off, and a broad, easy stairway of stone winds up to the paved platform on which the church stands, just as it might have done on any natural mound rising sharply out of the plain.

About half a mile away is a cone of rather similar shape and greater height, and one wonders how any race could take up the notion of erecting a huge artificial structure requiring prodigious labor, when right at hand is a " high place" ready made for worship or other use. I could see no place whence such an enormous bulk of earth could have been taken, for this mass is now one thousand feet at the base, and its razed top is a platform one hundred and sixty-five feet square, at a height of two hundred and four feet. Still, learned writers think that this hill is artificial, was once terraced and built on, forming a *pueblo* or village on its sides, with a *teocallis* or temple on top.

Cholula, said to have been a great city when first reached by the Spaniards, is now a straggling village of, one would think, two or three thousand souls. It has a forlorn look now, but its churches, standing and in ruins, indicate important religious establishments here at some time. The remains of the old Franciscan Monastery fronting the plaza, with the churches and gardens and closes connected, make the most delightful subjects for the painter; and I would undertake to easily furnish half a dozen water-colorists with bits of this one huge pile enough to make them a successful season in the exhibitions.

This monastery was founded in 1529; and what lives of huge satisfaction the old monks must have led here for more than three hundred years, away from all turmoil of the world, their existence almost hidden, no troublesome Protestant to fret, no prying interviewer to report, tithes duly paid, garden and glebe duly worked by dusky peons, all days bright with sunshine and sweet with flowers, all nights lulled by the nightingales, from all parts of the fair plain, stretching away on every hand to the great hills, the music of sweet chapel bells, great Popocatapetl and Ixtaccihuatl pointing to heaven with shining fingers!

After dining in the car as usual went by tramway to Tlascala. Population four thousand, and capital of the little state of same name. Pass through Santa Ana, where is a most charming little church with a fine bell-tower on one side of the front and a clock-tower on the other. The Tlascalans became allies of Cortez on his way to Mexico, and by their help he captured that city. Consequently he favored them, and in the municipal building are shown tokens of it, such as a handsomely illuminated parchment conveying a grant of arms to Tlascala, signed by Charles Fifth, the standard given by Cortez to the Tlascalan chiefs, the robes they wore when baptized, etc.

We filed, by invitation, into the Governor's reception-room, where we understood we should be received by him, but word was brought that his Excellency was unwell and not able to present himself. So it was thought to be the thing that one of our party should call on him in his sick-room—this was suggested by his secretary—and report to the party what the Governor was like and other particulars. I was chosen to represent the party, and was ushered into a suite of rooms connecting with the reception-room, where I was cordially received by his Excellency of Tlascala, who was fully dressed and walking about smoking a cigarette, showing no marks of illness. A little dappled fawn was disporting itself as a household pet through the rooms. The Governor is a full-blooded Indian of the same race as Juarez, with a strong and not unkindly face. Through Signor Rivaroll, our principal interpreter, he expressed his pleasure that our party had visited his city, and his regret that he could not personally show it some attention, and wished us a pleasant stay and prosperous journey. I replied that his friendly sentiments and good wishes were cordially reciprocated, and took leave with much hand-shaking. Passing through the room between the presence and the reception-room, a room with no bed in it, and seeming to be an ante-chamber to his Excellency's private apartment, I noticed a handsomely decorated utensil not commonly given a place of honor standing conspicuously on an inlaid stand as if an article of ornament. Señora Prospero Cahuantzl may not have advanced as far in æstheticism as her august spouse in politics. I reported to our party that his Excellency was a kindly man, not so ill-looking as his portrait hanging on the wall of the reception-room would indicate, that he wished the Raymond excursionists well, and did not intend either to roast or scalp the members of it at this time.

Visited the old Church of San Francisco, dating from 1521. It stands on a terraced hillside, and is approached by a wide paved way bordered by a double row of old trees, and under a triple archway that unites the bell-tower with the convent, now used as a barrack. The roof is upheld by richly carved red-cedar rafters and beams. There is a beautiful old altar.  In a chapel opening from the church is the stone pulpit from which the Christian faith was, it is said, first preached in the new world, as an inscription declares.  There is also shown the font in which the four Tlascalan chiefs whose portraits are in the Casa Municipal are said to have been baptized in 1520.  Here is an *Ecce Homo* of the most revolting description.  A life-size image of Christ is lying in a half-prostrate and most painful position with a score of bloody wounds, so that it is almost bathed in blood, the flesh worn through to the apparent bone at several points, about the neck a long rope, stained too with blood, making altogether an object so repulsive that it is difficult to understand how even the lowest order of mind can feel anything but utter loathing at the sight of it.

Our train ran back from Puebla, which is on a branch line of the Mexican Railroad, to Apizaco, thence on the direct line to Esperanza, where we lay (March 4th) until eight o'clock, the glorious cone of Orizaba rising free from clouds.  Here we left our Pullman cars, all except the dining-car being too long for the curves on the road down the mountain, and taking the day coaches of the Mexican Railroad, began the wonderful descent from the table-land to the coast, at Boca del Monte

("Mouth of the Mountain"), the next station below Esperanza. This is a few feet short of eight thousand feet above the level of the gulf. At Maltrata, just below, so that we look sheer down on it, although twelve and a half miles distant, as the road winds and doubles on itself, 2374 feet of descent has been made, and at Orizaba, twelve miles further on, fifteen hundred feet more, and at Paso del Macho, forty-five miles from Vera Cruz and two hundred and sixteen miles from the City of Mexico, the furthest point reached, we are within 1560 feet of the sea-level, having descended 6364 feet in fifty-six miles.

This road from Orizaba to Esperanza is regarded as one of the marvels of engineering. The engine used is called the Fairlie, a "double-ender," giving the force of two. We had an exceptionally fine day down. For several days before a "Norther" had prevailed from the direction of the Gulf, filling the mountains with fog, but to-day all was clear and beautiful in sky and air. Before reaching Orizaba the mountain of that name shone out grandly. It is something over seventeen thousand feet high, and at this point we were thirteen thousand feet below its top. The scenery all the way down is exceedingly grand. The track descends the steep grades by winding down along shelves on the mountain-sides, whence are seen far below, green vales running sharply to an end in the hollows of great hills clad in verdure to their very tops, sunless ravines at dizzy depths below with the flash of a cascade here and there out of the gloom, lofty mountain-peaks, also verdure-clad, little smiling plats and broader levels of cultivated land laid out in little squares, of alternate green and brown, like a chess-board, on which we look down almost perpendicularly, as, emerging from a tunnel, we crawl over an iron bridge so slender, across a gorge so deep, that we seem suspended in mid-air.

At Maltrata, which we approach on three sides before coming to the station, a great variety of fruit is brought by Mexican girls and offered at small prices—pineapples at ten cents each, and woven baskets, costing twenty-five cents at home, holding more than a peck of fine oranges, at twenty-five cents, basket and all.

From Orizaba we continue to descend among tropical vegetation to Paso del Macho, whence we return to Orizaba, where we remain an hour. Below this point, in a deep cut, a transverse tunnel, with just room enough to walk, leads to an open space with abundant vegetation and a beautiful cascade of a good deal of water falling say twenty-five feet into a wide basin, and at the hour we saw it a rainbow on the mist near the bottom—a charming sight. It is said the water comes from a subterranean source, and, after falling, again disappears, but I could not determine this.

Orizaba is delightfully situated, and were I compelled to live in Mexico would be the spot I should choose out of all I have seen. It is midway between the table-land and coast in altitude, and has the temperate advantages of both. The climate is said to be delightful all the year round, and the wealthy from Vera Cruz come here to escape the heat of the coast. The huge mountains which shut it in have a kindly, sheltering look and smile with green to their summits, and the fertile plain winds in and out among their feet and runs up into their ravines in the most pastoral and charming way.

We rode out into the country through orange groves and coffee plantations—luxuriant growths—through which wind sweet-scented lanes bordered with many strange and beautiful flowers. Here grow maize, tobacco, wheat, barley, coffee, sugar-cane, pineapples, bananas, oranges, lemons, limes, pomegranates, mangoes, tumas, graneditas, pitayas, aguacates, chirrimoyas, granadas, mameys, zapotes, chicos, and I know not what beside, and of course all the common vegetables. Tobacco I noticed largely cultivated up from Orizaba for several miles.

Climbed up to Esperanza and regained our own train, and leaving that station at one o'clock A.M., reached Mexico, on our return, at eight the same morning. As the train left Esperanza I awoke and had a full and fine view of the Southern Cross, then near the meridian. Its head was about twenty degrees above the southern horizon. It is not to be compared to the constellations which blaze in our northern winter skies. The Mexican Railroad was built by English money and engineers, and is solid and stanch like John Bull himself. The roadbed—a single track—is, I should say, not excelled by any one I ever rode on, and nothing short of the sturdiest pluck and skill could have contrived a way to lift trains from the low to the high regions up through these lofty mountains.

## CHAPTER XIV.

*The Iturbide Hotel and its cheerlessness—A chilly day—A paragraph about the bull-fight—A visit to the Cathedral and a description of its interior and its devotees—Take leave of Mexico with a few remarks on its past and present government—A ride through many places of interest.*

*March 5th.*—Breakfasted in car, and went to the Iturbide, a chill, cheerless prison of a hotel, and the Café Anglais, a dirty, tiresome eating-house. We live better on the train than anywhere we stop. There was shower enough last night to wet the streets quite thoroughly. All say this is unusual, and speak, too, of the cold, which, night and morning, is so considerable that at home we should not think of doing without fires. There is a special chill in the sunless rooms of this hotel. One of the regulations staring at me every time I pass along the stone hall is worth preserving :

"*Art.* 5*th.* No lodger is entitled to harbor one or more persons in his room or apartment without having first settled with the manager the sum he is to pay for the hiring of each of the extra beds which are to be afforded to the persons whom he has been willing to host. This letting may be bargained with the manager either by days, fortnights, or months, and as to the way of paying, the same course will be kept as concerning the payment for the letting of rooms or apartments."

The mercury showed forty-seven degrees at 8 A.M. The sun's rays are hot when they act directly, but in the shade it is chilly. The people do not act as if they cared for the cold, but must feel it, and Dr. Parsons informs me that in this unhealthiest city in the world pulmonary diseases head the list—not chronic, but acute—and among what he calls the "barefoot people." Spent some hours in the tiresome business of selecting photographs at Spaulding's.

Apropos of bull-fighting, I quote from the *Two Republics* of Monday last a paragraph of an article relating to the *toreador* Mazzantini, already alluded to—he acted at Puebla last Sunday : "As soon as Mazzantini made his appearance he was greeted by unstinted applause from fifteen thousand throats. Governor Marquez presided over the entertainment. Mazzantini's neat and effective work called out applause ranging from a Comanche yell to a new silk hat. Everything proceeded as smooth as an opera, and as the last bull staggered in his tracks the crowd filed out with *vivas* upon *vivas* for Mazzantini. In the evening the king of the bull-fighters was tendered a serenade by his admirers." I noticed two large rings well under way on the Avenue de la Reforma, making, with the one where I went last Sunday, three within the city limits.

*March 6th, Sunday.*—Went to the Cathedral to mass at 10 A.M. The enormous space was well filled with worshippers crowded closely here and there about the main altar, the Altar of Pardon, and the favorite shrines. Such groups! It seems to me that in no land under heaven can, in this age, so heterogeneous, strange, and picturesque a throng be gathered together in any great church. Kneeling familiarly side by side, without the least aversion on the one hand or avoidance on the other, were well-clad ladies and gentlemen and the vilest beggars in parti-colored rags, stately señoras and señoritas with glorious eyes and proud bearing, kissing the floor before some shrine where an instant before the dirty, naked foot or dirtier sandal of many a peasant from the country round or the poor of the city had pressed! I saw a well-dressed Spaniard in English clothes interrupt his prayers to kiss the floor, and noticing that he so caressed it with his lips as to leave a moist spot, I was interested to count, and found he already had made twenty-seven, and while I observed he increased the number to thirty. The stately figures of the swarthy and haughty ecclesiastics in their gorgeous vestments of gold and blue and purple formed a pleasing picture grouped about the great altar with their robed attendants, clouds of perfume from the swinging silver censers slowly filling all the air. Nothing could exceed the fervor of the worshippers. Before the altar-railings of the numerous chapels on each side of the Cathedral were kneeling groups frequently praying with passionate gesticulation, and fond looks directed to the tutelar saint carved or painted above the altar, in all the ecstasy of adoration. In each of the many confessionals of dark mahogany clamped with brass sat a priest with ear inclined to the little grated opening at which kneeling penitents whispered their confessions, with kneeling rows behind them, mostly women, patiently waiting their turn. As one venerable priest, aged and wrinkled, tottered to his seat in the confessional, several well-dressed and handsome Spanish ladies who were waiting for him came forward, and with respectful tenderness saluted him by taking his hand, bending low and kissing it long and fervently.

The dominion of the Church in Mexico was

well-nigh absolute from the time of the conquest, without check or impediment, until the severe shock it sustained through Juarez in 1861, who procured the secularization of all Church property, the disbanding and unhousing of all religious orders and societies of every kind whatsoever, including even the Sisters of Charity, and the introduction of religious toleration and the equality of all sects before the law. Up to that time more than one half the wealth of the republic was owned by the Church, and as it always opposed all movements in favor of greater liberty, it was all through the trying years of the change from monarchy to democracy the most serious obstacle to success.

Richard H. Dana, in his "Two Years Before the Mast," relates that in 1834 no one could expect to live in Mexico and do business unless he was a Catholic, and previous to that time, in any town or city, the stranger who should fail to drop on his knees with uncovered head when a procession passed would have been pretty sure of being mobbed by the populace. Now processions are forbidden in the streets, nor can any ecclesiastic appear abroad in clerical garb. The priests have been deprived of a great body of their sacerdotal functions—even their marriages are not legal unless accompanied by civil sanction, and so absolutely has the State possessed itself of all ecclesiastical property that even the churches proper are occupied by their congregations as tenants at will.

Rode on the Paseo with Betty from four to six, the fashionable hours. The pavement is watered by porters who dash jars of water over it in a dexterous way from the bordering ditches, and with their broad straw hats, white tunics, and trousers rolled well up over their handsome bronze legs, make a not unpleasing feature of the promenade.

*March 7th.*—A.M. made some purchases. At 5 P.M. left fair Mexico City by the Mexican Central, on our return to El Paso. On taking leave of our most interesting sister republic, one cannot help wondering what its future is likely to be. It does not seem easy to forecast it. While nominally a republic with a constitution modelled upon that of the United States, Mexico is really a military oligarchy, the head of which is a President backed by an army of sixty thousand men and supported by a compact body of from four to six thousand landholders, who possess nearly all the land of the republic, keep it free from taxation, and hold the laborers by a modified form of peonage in almost as complete servitude as their ancestors were under Spanish rule.

The Congress really chosen by government

influence is the creature of the executive will, and is in no sense the representative of the ten millions of people, who take, for the most part, no interest whatever in public affairs. The presidency has been the prize of ambitious generals and warring factions, and since its separation from Spain, in 1821, Mexico has had fifty-five presidents, two emperors, and one regency! Not until 1848 was the presidency peaceably transferred. At that time General Arista succeeded General Herrera without violence; but Arista was banished two years after, and within three months there were four presidents.

Pretty much all the great leaders in the war of independence were put to death by their own people, so were both emperors and two presidents, while most of the others were either banished or obliged to go into exile to save their lives. Ex-President Gonzales, who at the end of his term peacefully gave place to his successor, General Diaz, now President, is said to have taken the office in debt and to have retired at the end of one term worth anywhere from fifteen to twenty million dollars.

The political career of General Diaz well illustrates my meaning. He was distinguished in the army, was General-in-Chief of the force which recovered the capital from Maximilian in 1866, offered himself as a candidate for the presidency in 1871, was defeated by Juarez, refused to accept the result because, as he held, the re-election of a president was unconstitutional, issued a manifesto, raised a force, and after a sanguinary war of several months was fully defeated, was amnestied, lived peacefully at the capital until 1876, then rebelled against Lerdo, who became President on the death of Juarez, defeated him, captured the capital, assumed the presidency, and had these lawless proceedings ratified by a so-called popular election. It is said he will not voluntarily give up his office. He is a man of ability, is believed really to have the good of his country at heart, is liberal in his views, encourages enterprises, education, the arts; and many whom I conversed with insisted he is the best of the presidents, and gives as good a government as the condition of affairs will permit.

The people are poor, and the natural resources of the country, not as great as is generally supposed, imperfectly developed. Spain, through its viceroys, kept it impoverished by an ingenious and exhaustive system of taxation, the Church clutched the greater part of what remained, during the bloody wars for independence and the civil strifes which followed lawlessness and brigandage prevailed, wealth forsook the country, industries and improvements were laid waste, and, lastly, a neighboring republic, as the result of what I regard as a most unjust war, seized by the strong hand the richest half of its territory and left the remainder impoverished, torn, and bleeding.

One third of its population of ten millions are native Indians of unmixed blood, speaking the language of their fathers, living as they lived, and, except in some notable instances, without aspirations for anything better, apathetic, inoffensive, contented. A million or so are of European blood, the Spanish greatly predominating, the remainder of Spanish and Indian blood mingled confusedly in all degrees. These things do not promise well, yet there is a national life and positive progress. The stifling grasp of the Church is loosened from the republic's throat. Science and the arts have a sure footing and a free growth, education spreads, and presages of a better future abound. Surely in all these aspirations our strong nation might well aid a sister republic, its next neighbor, struggling toward light and freedom.

*March 8th.*—Woke at Silao. Rode steadily all day in the dust and heat. Mercury showed seventy-eight degrees on the shady side of the car at 3 P.M. Had fine views of Zacatecas and Guadalupe from the hill as we approached them. Some one found a copy of the El Paso

*Times* of the 6th having a telegram from New York, dated the 5th inst., that Henry Ward Beecher had a stroke of apoplexy and would not probably recover.

*March 9th.*—Woke at Lerdo on the southern border of the long strip of desert. Bought a basket of strawberries and hulled them for breakfast. A hot, dusty, dreary ride all day. Reached Chihuahua at 7 P.M. and El Paso at 9 A.M.

*March 10th.*—After slight examination of baggage and waiting all day, left for California at 7 P.M. by the Southern Pacific Railway, and rode all night.

*March 11th.*—Woke at a little station in the desert land of Arizona, reaching Tucson at 9 A.M., where we remained two hours, then on over the most dreary country one can imagine. Heat at 3 P.M. ninety degrees. Dust and dreariness, and drouth everywhere. At 6 P.M. reached Yuma, on the Colorado River, here about ten rods wide as seen by moonlight, and navigable for small steamboats; then on again, after an hour's wait.

*March 12th.*—Near Colton, Cal., where we were cheered by the sight of spaces made green by irrigation, something like a continuity of verdure extending from the valley up the hills, and water here and there. Came into the fertile and prosperous San Gabriel Valley, reaching Los Angeles, grown in a year or two from ten thousand to forty-five thousand, at 12 M.

Went by a branch road eight miles to Pasadena, to the Raymond, where we were glad to meet all the comforts of a first-class hotel, managed by Merrill of the Crawford House, White Mountains. Its two hundred rooms have been filled all winter, and it was with difficulty we got accommodations. The situation is delightful, on an eminence sloping every way and looking over the lovely valley of the San Gabriel, stretching, as a wide plain, to the same kind of hills we have had ever since we entered Mexico a month ago, except that in places on these there are patches of green. On some of the highest peaks is snow, not perpetual, but remaining from the fall of last month, and will remain, it is said, into July. The valley is of great fertility, made so by irrigation from streams from the mountains and in places by artesian wells. Here, as in Mexico and all this country, deserts bloom at the touch of water, as it were an enchanter's wand. Not easily can one tire of looking out from the piazzas of the Raymond upon the varied landscape below, steeped in a semi-tropical atmosphere.

## CHAPTER XV.

*We pass an enjoyable day at the Hotel Raymond—Take a long drive to the Sunny Slope Winery—"Lucky Baldwin" and his ranch—We visit Los Angeles and then ride to "Kinneyloar," the residence of a retired New York cigarette-maker—Leave for 'Frisco—Golden Gate Park—A drive through Chinatown.*

*March* 13*th, Sunday.*—Passed a delicious day at the Raymond. A fine company of guests here, much as is met at any very best hotel at the East, and from many cities and States.

*March* 14*th.*—A.M. took a long drive to the Sunny Slope Winery owned by Rose & Stern, and lately put into a new style, "The Rose Wine Co., Limited." Rose owns a great tract of land in oranges, lemons, walnuts, olives, etc., but chiefly in vines and wheat, of which, it is said, he has five thousand acres now growing, and I do not know how many of vines. They crush two hundred tons of grapes a day in the season, using not only their own, but lots they buy of growers who raise to sell. Went through their cellars, now mostly empty, where are many casks said to hold five thousand gallons each. We tasted a fairish wine called port, and the clerk in charge recommended a white wine called burger, a bottle of which I ordered at lunch at the Raymond, and found not at all to my liking; excessively acid and fiery.

Our ride lay through great orchards of oranges laden heavily with the golden fruit, plantations of apricots, peaches, and almonds, now in blossom, groves of walnuts, etc., in many cases enclosed in hedges of clipped Monterey cypress, forming the closest and prettiest fences imaginable, with roads bordered by rows of the fast-growing eucalyptus, pepper-trees, and California oaks, which are much like the water-oaks of Florida and Texas.

Rode through E. J. Baldwin's farm, or ranch, as farms are called here, of fifty-seven thousand acres. He is also called "lucky Baldwin"—not, it is probable, from his matrimonial escapades, he now being sixty-three years old, it is said, and having had seven wives, four still living, and the acknowledged one but seventeen years old, but from the fortunate turn his real-estate operations have taken.

We returned to the hotel through Pasadena, a pretty village of embowered cottages, the growth of little more than one year, and now the subject of a "boom" of exceeding vigor. A plot of land at the intersection of two principal streets, sixty by two hundred and twenty-five feet, is said, on good authority, to have been sold a day or two ago for one thousand dollars a foot, or sixty thousand dollars. The air is delicious, soft, yet cool, bracing, and tonic. Our driver said it was not much different all winter, and as we passed a school-house with the boys out at play, barefoot, he said, "That is the way they go all winter."

*March 15th.*—All day at Raymond.

*March 16th.*—Drove to Los Angeles, eight miles, a handsome town with a city look, said to have grown from ten to forty-five thousand in less than five years. Business streets substantially built and a good deal of activity shown. The town has tramways worked by horses, cable, and electricity. It lies pleasantly on the river of the same name, and is likely to become the principal city of Southern California. The roads are deep with dust in most places, but are not at all as bad as they will be later, it is said, when, except where irrigation is possible, all will be brown desolation.

*March 17th.*—P.M. drove to "Kinneyloar," the residence of a retired cigarette-maker in New York, who, with much labor and expense and considerable taste, has made himself a home, with fine orange groves, etc., close up to a sharp rise of the Sierra Madre, here mounting up something over four thousand feet. He is on a platform about eight hundred feet above the plain, as is the neighboring Sierra Madre Villa, a hotel well spoken of, but, with the exception of a fine lawn—having that rarest of all things here except water, smooth, solid, green turf—bearing no comparison to the Raymond.

*March 18th.*—Left for 'Frisco at 1 P.M. Crossed the Sierra Madre Range and the Mohave Desert, and woke,

*March 19th*, in the San Joaquin Valley, amid great fields of young wheat and other spring crops such as one is more accustomed to at the East, or more particularly in the West and North-west. This valley contains seven million acres and resembles a Western prairie, and all along are far more signs of agricultural prosperity than we have seen since leaving home.

Reached Oakland at 11 A.M., passing along the south-west shore of Benicia Bay, the south shore of the strait connecting it with San Francisco Bay and the east and south shore of the bay itself. The whole view along is pleasing, the hills back of Benicia and all the land about clad in verdure, and the water of 'Frisco Bay, as we crossed it by ferry from Oakland, a rich green, and everything soft and mellow in the hazy light.

The city itself is rather disappointing as

approached from the water, filling the level land in a dull, crowded way, without picturesque features to catch the eye, straggling up the abrupt heights behind in a rambling sort of way, and showing to the north great, ugly patches of brown slope. Our party was booked for the Palace Hotel, and we had been promised choice rooms there, but those shown me were so poor that I refused them and came to the Baldwin.

*March* 20*th.*—Went to the church of Dr. Spinner, who was once in Kalamazoo over the Presbyterian Church there. He was absent, trying the effect of a change of climate for obstinate neuralgia. The day is warm and sunny. I saw placards on the wall advertising two different picnic parties. The streets have a Sunday look, although I notice many stores open, of one kind and another. P.M. went to Golden Gate Park, made with great pains, taste, and use of much money, on the sandy upland about half way to the Cliff. It contains fourteen hundred acres, well laid out in grass and evergreens, of which only about one third is under improvement, and to reach the Pacific, some four miles away, when completed. The red earth of the walks and drives comes from two hills near by, and is of such a sort that I am told it needs no mixing with anything to make a driveway so firm as to suggest a cement road-bed, and contrasts agreeably with the verdure.

The drive was thronged with carriages, as were the walks with orderly people, mostly of a plain sort, much like those seen on fine Sundays in Central and Prospect Parks. I was struck here as elsewhere with the healthy, vigorous look of the women, who seem to prosper in this climate. The proportion of well-looking and even handsome faces seems to me greater here than in any city I know. They surpass the men in their appearance of freshness and vigor.

Access is had to this park by a line of cable-cars. These are in common use here, and there is an excellent system of them covering all directions and used generally, I should say, by all sorts of the people. They run, of course, as fast as the cables which they grasp, and let go at the will of the engineer on each, who readily starts and stops them, and they move uniformly at about the speed of a moderate trot. The only irregularity is a quick movement as the grip clutches the cable, which is hidden underground and reached through a groove running parallel with the rails and between them. They move up-hill and down at the same rate of speed, and go right up the steep face of the cliffs, rising abruptly in all directions from the city, except where it fronts the bay.

*March 21st.*—P. M. drove through Chinatown, consisting of several blocks in the heart of the business part of the city, occupied almost wholly by Chinese, and presenting externally a much less squalid and repulsive appearance than I expected from what I had read and heard. Many of the men are much superior in physique, looks, and bearing to those of their nation in New York, for instance, and I was surprised to find such fine, costly, and rare stocks of Chinese and Japanese goods on sale in their stores, and still more to meet such bright, smart-looking, pleasant salesmen.

In one of them was a little girl say ten years old, daughter of the proprietor, whose feet had undergone the bandaging process, so that her little ornamented shoes would not go on the feet of an ordinary American child of three years, the compression having reduced the toes and front of the foot to a short, narrow lump, so destroying the elasticity of the foot and narrowing its base that she walked with a tottering, sinuous motion, almost painful to see.

The Chinese are capital salesmen, speak fair English, are quick to see your intentions and wants, very polite, and skilful in praising their goods. They show beautiful goods in porcelain, ivory, and bronze, rich embroideries, crape shawls, etc., and stand so well by the prices they make as not to offend with the idea that they are cheating, and succeed well in impressing one with the notion of their candor and fairness. Their goods seem cheap compared with New York prices. There are some who do a jobbing business, and some who sell altogether at wholesale. Among those we called on are Wing Chong Lung & Co., 617 Dupont Street; Kim Lung Co., 723 Dupont Street; Chy Lung & Co., 640 Sacramento Street, and Chin Lee Co., 521 Kearney Street.

We went to a leading restaurant and had each a cup of tea, very good, and made each in its cup by pouring hot water on the leaves and covering the cup for a moment with a tiny saucer, and then pouring it into a still smaller cup for drinking. With it came a plate of partly dried pits of a sort of almond, a plate of preserved ginger, and a rough, thorny shell, covering what looked like a dried grape, of a sharpish and not agreeable taste with a single seed looking like a vanilla bean.

## CHAPTER XVI.

*The Cliff House—Sea-lions and their haunts—A sight of Chinatown at night—Its streets, its shops, and the character of its inhabitants—The opium dens—Go to a Chinese theatre and witness a performance, after which we enter a Joss-house and make observations.*

*March 22d.*—Went out to the Cliff House on the north-west point of the cape on which the city stands, at the south side of the entrance to the Golden Gate, as the strait is called leading into San Francisco Bay, about as wide, I should say, or a little wider than The Narrows at the entrance to New York Harbor. To the west is the broad Pacific, its deep blue pulsations coming lazily up on a sloping, sandy beach and stretching away without limit toward the Orient under an opaline sky.

Twenty rods off the craggy rocks on which the Cliff House is built are five precipitous rocks of unequal size rising from the sea, haunted by seals, called here sea-lions, presumably because this is a more startling name for these uncouth, repulsive amphibia. There are more than a hundred of them making a home on these rocks, when resting in the sun from the joy and labor of the waves, where they gambol and find their daily food, easily catching all the fish they want, and being protected from hunters by the laws. The 'Friscans are proud of them as one of the attractions of the city, and their right to the solace of sun and rock there is prescriptive, and runneth far beyond the memory of the "forty-niner." They take their food in the morning. We watched them coming in and climbing up the steep, bare crags with painful but effective clumsiness, and forcing those already crowding the secure places to make room in a commotion of twisting necks, wabbling fins, and hoarse, abrupt barks, something between that of a mastiff dog and the preliminary *brool* of a lion.

At 7 P.M. Mr. Vale came for me to make the round of Chinatown by night. Went to the old City Hall police station and were taken in charge by Sergeant Houghtaling, a "forty-niner," from Peekskill, N. Y., and an officer in this precinct for many years, and so fully familiar with all about it. There were five in the party —all men. We set out about eight o'clock, and I reached my hotel at 1 A.M., well tired out with nearly five hours on foot.

We looked into the Orientals' shops of various sorts and found them exceedingly interesting.

They buy and use almost nothing made or grown here, and so far as possible live completely apart from Americans in all respects. They have their own drug-stores, for example, in which prescriptions of their own native doctors are compounded. Their pharmacopœia is extensive, and consists chiefly of plants, including roots, leaves, barks, and gums. I was told they use no minerals. I saw several prescriptions filled, and the doses would seem to be heroic, but as they compound the crude materials, bulk may be only an incident. They also use animal medicines, which they import nicely prepared and give by decoction—lizards for dyspepsia, locusts for weak eyes, snakes for rheumatism. Beetles and cockchafers, too, come within the domain of the learned profession of medicine in the oldest nation in the world. Their groceries come from China, and are of great variety. Rice is the staple, and dried and preserved fruits and vegetables, to an extent beyond anything we know, fill the grocers' shelves in the snuggest, neatest, and most ingenious parcels, wrapped and secured to an extent that, with the price of labor with us, would cost more than the articles themselves. Besides, they bring meats and fresh vegetables by steamer from China, and so cheap are they at home, that, the sergeant informs me, they reach here cheaper than they can be grown and sold here. I was shown ten varieties of potatoes—queer, exaggerated tubers they were too—huge fresh citrons, ducks dried in the sun and preserved in oil, dried oysters, dried pigs' and ducks' livers, the queerest sausages, dried codfish with great, round heads and goggle eyes, like those drawn for dolphins in old engravings, huge hampers of eggs boiled hard and encased each in a firm, thick coating of mud, and a huge metal jar in which live catfish were swimming about—all come from China by steamer.

The variety of all this is bewildering, and beyond the wonder that such common articles should be imported into a country prolific as this coast is in the necessaries of life, it shows how utterly they keep themselves apart from us. They even import their poultry. Nothing is lost or wasted. A chicken had just been killed in one of the groceries we visited, and its blood was saved in a cup to be sent to the customer; and I was told the entrails would be carefully washed and cooked and eaten. All these articles were clean, great care being used in the processes and the handling, and, from the Mongolian point of view, carefully and neatly done.

We then visited many opium dens and saw a

great number of men who had finished their suppers getting ready for sleep after a smoke of opium. It costs about ten cents' worth of opium to produce the sleep, the smoker filling his pipe two or three times, and consuming each charge by three or four inhalations. It is quite a knack to prepare the pipe for smoking. This is a wide, shallow bowl of metal with a bamboo stem two feet long. The opium is a black paste; is carefully put in the bowl, a hole is made through it, then, holding it top down over the flame of a lamp already burning at his side, the Chinaman lies down with all his clothing on except his hat and shoes, rests his head on the short, oblong block of wood which serves him for a pillow, takes a long inhalation, drawing the smoke down deep into the lungs and slowly emitting it from the nostrils. Two or three of these inhalations consume the opium, and after a moment's waiting he charges his pipe again, an operation requiring, I should say, five minutes. The effect seems to be prompt, and two or three such smokes to suffice, when, putting out his lamp or leaving it for a co-tenant of the platform which serves for a bed to as many as can lie on it, he falls into a deep slumber, from which he can be roused with difficulty, lasting till morning. Then he wakes, eats his breakfast, and goes about his day's labor—his hours being, when driven by work, from 6 A.M. to midnight—to repeat his smoking the next night, and so on. This is done not in public rooms for the purpose, but in the rooms, or more properly holes, where they swarm to an extent incredible to one who does not see it with his own eyes.

In a room, seven by twelve feet, reached by going down two flights of stairs below ground, were twenty-seven men in bed. They had cooked and eaten quite an elaborate supper of several dishes there. This stowing is done by putting up shelves or platforms one above another against the wall on one side, with only space enough to crawl in, where they lie like herrings in a box, as the sergeant expressed it. Still more marvellous are some of the statements of the sergeant of the packing done in rooms and houses, exceeding anything existing in the most crowded Caucasian abodes. The fact that within the compass of little more than, say, two squares of New York bounded on the east and west by Third and Fourth avenues is a population estimated at fifty thousand, speaks conclusively of the swarms in this Asiatic hive.

This is in a quarter of the old city, and the exterior architecture has not been greatly changed. Some of the fronts of the old buildings have been altered into conformity with the notions of the occupants, for stores, theatres, restaurants, etc., balconies, wooden awnings, and projections here and there thrown out; but the general character of the streets is unchanged; and the interiors of all the buildings are literally like the cells and passages of a beehive stuffed with comb. They put up innumerable partitions and cut the rooms in the old houses into dark cells and dens of all sorts, from garret to basement, down into cellars and sub-cellars and out under the sidewalks, where they wallow in unspeakable stench and foulness.

There are said to be but fourteen hundred women in all the colony, and these, almost without exception prostitutes, are said to be really slaves, and to be let and sold by their owners, the most attractive changing hands, sometimes at a valuation of about fifteen hundred dollars. These are not found in the crowded quarters, where the men swarm, as described above, but mostly in houses giving on narrow alleys, where they sit on the ground floor looking out of little square windows about four feet from the sidewalk, and ogle the passers-by—not so flagrantly, however, as may be seen on many streets of our large cities by night or day. They are poor, painted creatures with dull, sad faces, and look, as they are really, the soulless creatures of man's lust.

We went on the stage of the principal theatre by a series of tortuous, dark, narrow passages and stairways, and saw a small fraction of a play whose scene is laid two thousand years ago, the sergeant explained, and has been running now for four nights, and has just fairly begun. No one knows how long this will run. The sergeant said that an historical play just taken off ran four months—by which I mean the play took four months to act to the end. The performance begins at 4 P.M. and lasts till 12 midnight. There is no pretence of stage illusion, no scenery, no drop-curtain, no footlights, but, instead, gaslights from above. A free-and-easy orchestra sits on the back of the stage making a discordant clang-clang and tum-tum. During the half hour we were there five performers were on the stage—two females, one of high rank, a terrible old man, made up greatly like the Mikado in the opera of that name, and a young peasant leading a cow —the latter done by a youth with no pretence of likeness except his head thrust into a good imitation of a cow's head. The sergeant said the plot was of a poor peasant who came, by the favor of a young lady of rank, to be governor of a province. The female parts are taken by males; and the heroine of this play simpered and tottered and was made up, in hair and paint and costume, to look for all the world like such of their women as I had seen, and, with her falsetto voice, had the highest wages of any of a company of one hundred and twenty performers. These are all boarded in the building, and are stowed away as I have noted elsewhere.

In the midst of the play a performer went to a post at one side of the front of the stage and hung on a hook a brown placard freshly painted in Chinese characters. This signified that some one in the audience was wanted outside, and presently he came forward, took down the notice, and departed. As we passed out we were shown a rich robe in the property-room, stiff with gold embroidery, and in the greenroom was the manager painting his face white, streaked with ferocious black, being soon to go on the stage as a great general.

We went next to a Joss-house, a large hall in a second story with several shrines to as many deities, whose statues were rather richly set in niches with lights and perfumes before them. These images were not unpleasing in feature and aspect, and all I saw represented mortals deified for the abundance of their good deeds done in life. One was of a physician of great benevolence to the poor, and a much-cherished one dear to women in sorrow is that of an empress centuries agone, the inscription over whose head the sergeant interpreted, " Worshipped for her goodness in returning good for evil." The worship would seem to be quite perfunctory. The devout drop in at will, and, with one or more prostrations, burn a paper with a prayer on it, and go about their affairs. But suppose the Oriental mind through the visible image discovers the virtue it stands for, and beyond that a dim aspect of the invisible First Cause, where is the idolatry? Does the dissenting parson in the " meeting-house" have such indubitable views of the Eternal One that he can condemn all who do not share them to remediless perdition?

## CHAPTER XVII.

*Arrive at Monterey—Go to the Hotel del Monte and see its famous park—Leave for Santa Cruz—The big trees—A good climate for invalids—Napa, and the Napa Soda Springs Hotel—The charming Napa Valley—A ride to the Geysers—We describe them — Something about Charley Foss, the whip.*

*March 23d.*—P.M. went by rail to Monterey, down the beautiful Santa Clara Valley, and to the Hotel del Monte, famous for its park of one hundred and fifty acres or so in which it stands. These grounds are set with fine old trees, great pines, and Spanish oaks. One of the latter, I should say, spreads over a space one hundred and fifty feet in diameter. Fine turf has been made all under these trees and throughout the everglades with much labor and cost; and banks and parterres of flowers abundant and rich are all about, and with the summer air and freshness of all nature in sight—art being used, so that "nothing common or unclean" offers itself—make a charming spot difficult to leave.

*March 24th.*—We had a fine drive after four horses, "Alec" being the whip, who had driven six years in the Yosemite, and is, I should say, one of the originals in that profession. He had a peculiar vocabulary. He said to Betty, to dissuade her from stopping to get some short-stemmed, wild poppies, " Them posies grow so low that a bumble-bee would graze his shins stoopin' down to get the honey out." Our way was along the south side of the bay of Monterey, then winding back round the point, and returning along the north shore of a charming little winding bay and through great pine woods—a ride of nineteen miles, and all made on the land of the Southern Pacific Railroad Co., who own the hotel also. We had fine views of the Pacific from cliffs on which white-crested breakers dashed, of a richer green than I had seen before. Off-shore were crags haunted by seals climbing on the rocks, and numerously swimming about in the surf—this being their feeding-time of day.

*March* 25*th.*—Left at 6 A.M. by rail for Santa Cruz on the north side of the bay of Monterey, about twenty miles across by water, but some forty miles by rail. The country on the way is delightful, including the Pajaho Valley, and as we approached Santa Cruz, level, fertile, broad lands stretched away sheer to the Pacific, green, and fringed with a hard beach of fine white sand. We had a cottage on the grounds of the

Pope House, and went with four horses nine miles up the San Lorenzo River to the big trees. The ride up the river is very interesting and picturesque, the bottom of the wild cañon through which it runs being in places seven hundred feet below the roadway scooped out along its side. At last we wound down to its level, forded it, and were among the redwood trees in a fertile stretch of valley on the east bank. There are many trees of large size, but none equal to their more famous relatives of the Yosemite. The " Giant" measures sixty feet round, and is said to be two hundred and ninety feet high, and others are nearly as large. Santa Cruz has a population estimated at five thousand, is charmingly situated, but at present poorly built. It is well spoken of as to its climate for invalids, and it has fogs from the sea—said not to be harmful—that furnish moisture to the crops all about here.

*March 26th.*—Returned to Oakland, and thence by rail to Napa, crossing the Sacramento at Vallejo. The river here just above its mouth at Mare Island is nearly the width of the Hudson at Hoboken, and continues about the width of the latter as far up as one can see. At Vallejo took the cars for Napa, twenty miles up the valley of that name, thence by stage six miles to the Napa Soda Springs Hotel up among the hills two thousand feet. The Napa Valley is charming at this time of year, with its tender green of blade and leaf, and stretches out widely, between hills on the west and east, a broad, fertile plain of deep alluvium, very like, as all these valleys are, to the smaller and richer prairies of the West.

*March 27th.*—This is a pleasant spot, with fine views to the south down the Napa Valley and sheltered northward by the tops of a mountain range, on the flank of which are the springs and hotel. This latter is curious in being an exactly circular building, with the private apartments opening from an interior passage running all round, and a great parlor filling the central space under a high dome. It is said to have been intended originally for a stable and turned into a hotel, which is not only unique, but convenient and pleasant. The springs here are named "soda," and are so with differences, each having a slightly different flavor imparted by some other ingredient, so that one of the three is called the Lemonade Spring, from a weak, acidulous taste. The water is agreeable, and, as in the case of other springs over the country, great claims are made for their sanitary properties, stress being laid on the efficacy of the water in disorders of the stomach. It is bottled charged with its own gas, so that it will expel the cork, and sent all along the Pacific coast in great quantities as a table water and to drink with wines, for which it is said to be specially fitted. It can be freely drunk with impunity.

*March* 28*th*.—Left wife and the children at 8.30 A.M. to go to the Geysers, reached by returning to Napa, thence by rail to Calistoga, forty-six miles from 'Frisco, thence by stage twenty-six miles over the Mayacamas Mountains, on the north side of which are those wonderful phenomena known as the Geysers. The stage ride over the mountains is one of the few remaining famous mountain routes, and I was desirous of making it under as favorable conditions as possible.

Was disappointed in not riding over the road to the Geysers with Charley Foss, the son of the renowned Clark Foss, the co-rival of Hank Monks, who drove Horace Greeley on his famous ride from Reno down to Placerville. Both these worthies have bowled off out of sight to the " dim Plutonian shore," where, let us hope, they have the good company of the elder Weller and his grandson Tony (who early gave presage of future distinction in the profession by spurning the pint-pot and absolutely refusing any modicum less than a quart), and all good brethren of the whip in all ages, from Phaeton down. Monday was an off day for Charley, but there is likelihood we shall have him on our return, which will be still better, as the descent is greater.

Charley Foss owns the road built by his father nearly thirty years since, at a cost of thirty-five thousand dollars, and owned by him, stock and all, whereon for twenty-five years his pride was to bowl down the steep mountain road with four, six, and even eight horses. We had Foss's best driver to the Geysers, and after nine miles of almost level road from Calistoga along through the Napa Valley to its upper end, then through Knight's Valley, reached by climbing over a ridge separating it from Napa Valley, and of the same fertile and level soil, and said to be worth one hundred dollars per acre for farming purposes, we began the ascent of the mountain ten miles to the summit, thirty-two hundred feet above the sea, thence down to the Pluton, the stream on which the Geysers are, six miles, descending in that distance seventeen hundred feet. The views up and down are broad and grand.

*March 29th.*—Was awakened at half-past five to visit the Geysers. Started with guide and four others. The Pluton, a clear mountain stream, flows down a cañon of steep walls, three hundred and fifty feet deep in places, but with a wide, level bank on the south, where the Geyser Hotel stands.  It here flows to the north-west, and contracting its banks again into a deep cañon, goes on for sixteen miles to Cloverdale, and loses itself in the Russian River.  Just opposite the hotel a narrow ravine opens from the stream almost at right angles and runs a little way back, where it loses itself between hills of crumbled, pasty rock, bare of all vegetation, streaked in dull yellow, red and gray, and having a general appearance of having been pulverized and worked over and over.  Crossing the Pluton by going through a bathing-house, where natural hot sulphur vapor baths are given, we entered this ravine and found ourselves at once in what easily seemed to me a sort of devil's kitchen, getting ready for breakfast.  From hundreds of tiny fissures and holes on both slopes of the ravine issued steam, here in jets and violent puffs, and there in slow, continuous threads.  The uncanny phenomena thickened as we went on, until we were soon in the midst of a diabolical hissing, stewing, boiling, sputtering, and a cloud of steam charged with smells befitting.

Here is a pool of stiffish mud boiling sluggishly, near by a kettle of clear alum-water, close to it another of soda—these hollowed out in a ledge breast-high, as if set in a huge range ;

there a broad, circular pool of clear water bubbling noisily in the liveliest agitation, a pot of black fluid overflowing near by, called the Devil's Inkstand. All was activity and bustle below, as if the Plutonian cook had his fires well agoing, and all preparations well forward. A little below the top of the ravine on the right is a round hole a foot in diameter, from which, with an intermittent, sharp bark, precisely like that of a locomotive getting under way, rushes a column of hot steam, and has done so since man remembers, night and day, incessantly.

Breakfasted, and at eight began the return drive with Charley Foss, four horses to a stage and seven passengers. The ride to the summit, six miles, was interesting, following the cañon of the Pluton. Six miles down the horses were changed, and I rode the rest of the way on the box with Foss, a fine, manly man who takes his father's place as whip, and is now among the few remaining great ones. The way he handles four horses is a fine art. They are parts of himself, a sort of increase and extension of his own organs, as it were, moving obediently to his volition. Like everything else that is thoroughly well done, his driving seems simple and easy as you confine your attention to it alone; but when one notices that the road-bed all the way is no more than a shelf high up the winding side of the mountain, formed by excavating and blasting out a notch in its abrupt face; that below is a precipice hundreds of feet down, and above the sheer wall of the cut for the road; that this road winds and twists into turns so sharp as to be called the "hairpin" and other fit names; that only in a few places could two wagons pass each other by any means; that we go on the full run out on a bold promontory and seem about to gallop off into space and strike *terra firma* a half mile down; that just as one shuts his eyes and holds his breath for the leap the leaders swing round the point of a crag, and with a "Steady there, Dick," we are bowling along and down the side of the projection—one realizes the nerve, skill and training of man and beast.

Foss holds almost human relations with his horses. They understand every intonation of his voice, every difference in his touch of rein. He holds conversation with them, cracks jokes with them, and they seem half to understand and to be in hearty sympathy with his moods. "What is the matter, old Sweet Sixteen?" to his nigh wheeler, as he struck soonest into a gallop, "are you red-hot this morning?" and he caressed him with a soft down brush of the doubled lash, laughing heartily *with* the tough little fellow whom he had driven for twelve years.

At Calistoga, Foss asked me to his rooms close by his large, well-kept stables, where he lives alone since his wife died last December, leaving him a pretty little daughter whose picture he showed me with pride. He gave me a photograph of his father, who looks fit to be on the bench of the Supreme Court, and promised to send me one of himself when he has more taken. He would not accept any money, and when I insisted on leaving a silver dollar on the table "To buy the little girl a ribbon," he consented with the manner of a man who is not satisfied with himself. A manly man, with much mountain wisdom and the instincts of a gentleman.

Reached 'Frisco at half-past six and found wife and family well situated at the Palace Hotel, in rooms such as were promised by the Itinerary. In the evening took them partly through Chinatown, visited the theatre, drug-store, grocery, and had tea in the best restaurant —a superb one too.

# CHAPTER XVIII.

*Bound for home—Stop on our way at Sacramento, where we are entertained by the city—Off again, and after travelling through miles of country of varied scenery, change at Ogden, and enter Salt Lake City—Description of the city, and a few words about the Mormons and their peculiar institutions.*

*March 30th.*—At noon left for home by the Central Pacific in a special train of ten Pullman cars. We have a hotel car and all in it were of our party to Mexico. The whole party consists of about two hundred, made up of parts of several excursions collected in California. We left here earlier than usual, to be entertained by the city of Sacramento, ninety miles distant, where we found waiting at the station vehicles enough of one sort and another to take us all about the city. To our lot fell a high and long express-wagon, into which two seats had been put lengthwise, and enough getting in to pretty well fill up, we joined one of the processions the whole had split into, and so went about, much to the joy of groups of boys who collected in advance of our coming all along the route and cheered and cried out encouragingly and whooped and executed wild and frenzied dances, after the manner of the small boy when the neighborhood of his residence is invaded by any extraordinary spectacle.

As we rode in a cloud of dust, by the time we reached the Cemetery we were so overlaid with it that "earth to earth" might have been spoken over us had a priest been present in this dismal spot, where the big square lots are built up above the alleyways and curbed round with brick. The monuments are of the usual dreary sort, but Mark Hopkins, who is buried here, has a fine tomb in the form of a huge, ancient sarcophagus built of Scotch or Tennessee granite. His widow opens her house here to the public, who may come and see a gallery of paintings said, by the Sacramento *Record Union*, to be the finest in the country. They are a poor lot, without one of the first or many of the second order, and would seem to be the cullings of the Hopkins Gallery as it grew under the improving taste and fortune of the millionaire, who was in the early time here the partner of D. C. Huntington in a hardware-store. The old sign is said to be still in the old place. The brothers Crocker were also here at that time in the dry-goods trade, and Leland Stanford, too, in the grocery business. It is said they used to get together, in the long, dull evenings, in each other's stores, and talk about a railroad to the East, until the notion took form, and with great nerve and skill they built the Central Pacific.

We lodged in our car at the station, and after dining there and clearing off the dust, went in the more humble way of a street-car—still at the expense of the city—to the State Capitol, which we found shining inside and out with electric light, and a good band discoursing from a stand on the turf by the main entrance. A committee took a good deal of civil pains in showing us over the building, a convenient one, with large, commodious, well-proportioned rooms, and said to have cost the State $2,500,000.

Sacramento has 27,000 population, is fairly built, and has a prosperous appearance, with a subdued air, as if a little fallen from some previous state of greater prosperity. It is said to be malarial, and its low situation would seem to indicate this. It is the centre of a magnificent country, the great valley of the Sacramento River stretching away on every hand as we came along, fertile and teeming like the richest of Western prairies.

*March* 31*st*.—Left Sacramento at seven A.M., and after crossing the American River, climbed the Sierra Nevada Mountains, crossing by a pass seven thousand feet high, through " Gold

Run" and "Dutch Flat," little, squalid mining hamlets left stranded by the retreating tide of mining fortunes, round Cape Horn, where there is a fine view two thousand feet sheer down to the American River winding through its gorges. The scenery all along is fine and only surpassed by that on the line of the Mexican National on the way down to Vera Cruz. Near the little station of Bronco we cross the Nevada line and traverse that State for four hundred and fifty miles. The greater part of the way is over a desert plain where nothing grows but the wild sage, where no water is nor can be unless from artesian wells bored at too great cost for private enterprise—as desolate and barren as anything in Mexico or Arizona. Just east of Tacoma, seven hundred miles from San Francisco, we enter Utah, and one hundred and thirty further on reach Ogden at 7 A.M.

*April 2d.*—Change at Ogden to the narrow-gauge track of the Denver and Rio Grande, down through the fertile valley of Salt Lake to Salt Lake City, in full view of the lake and the high, snow-covered mountains of the Wahsatch range, and are comfortably lodged at the Walker House in Salt Lake City.

*April 2d.*--The city of Salt Lake is situated in a basin of the same name—all at one time, it is probable, a salt lake or sea, now dry and fertile land, except Salt Lake—called by the Mormons the Dead Sea—without outlet, of about three thousand square miles and twenty-two per cent of salt in the water. The Jordan, a considerable fresh-water stream, taking its rise in Utah Lake, called by the Mormons the Lake of Galilee, twenty-two miles south of the city, discharges into it, and there are others, so that it is constantly fed by a great quantity of fresh water, and, so far as is known, the only escape for it is by evaporation. The city is located some ten miles from the head of the lake on a plain, but rising to the northeast by a gentle declivity, with many private residences, the business portion being on the nearly level land. There is descent enough, however, for rivulets of cool, fresh mountain water to run down the gutters of the streets in such volume as affords a constant refreshment to the eye.

The city is handsomely laid out in streets at right angles, one hundred and twenty feet wide, and while the population does not exceed thirty thousand, covers, I should say, one third the space of Mexico with its population of nearly three hundred thousand. This size comes not only from the great width of the streets, but still more from the number of small, comfortable houses, standing commonly each with a bit of land about it; so that, I should say, the people are as comfortably housed as in any town I know.

The business part is fairly well and solidly built, and there seems to be a good trade in a jobbing way. The Mormons, who are four fifths of the whole population, have their own co-operative store, where they buy at retail—a mercantile establishment of all kinds of merchandise on a great scale, like that of Loeser in Brooklyn.

The Walker is a very good hotel, with nearly as good cooking as we have found since leaving home. P.M. rode about the city. To the west are the lofty, serrated tops of the Oquirrh, and to the east and south the Wahsatch range, all well covered with snow now and will be until midsummer. A hundred miles away to the south rises in the clear air the cone of Mount Nebo, twelve thousand feet, and the site of Salt Lake is made noble and impressive by the giant mountain forms all about. Two miles east of the city is Camp Douglas, where our paternal Government maintains a regiment of infantry and some force of artillery, and half a mile south of this debouches into the plain the cañon whence issued the frenzied hordes of gold-seekers who, pouring into California in '49, reached this smiling valley destitute, famished and travel-worn from their dreadful journey overland. I thought of the little company of my schoolmates who set out so hopefully from Kalamazoo County, Mich., and struggled through with ox-teams and canvas-covered wagons—a great trial of human endurance.

Visited the Mormon Assembly House, intended for worship in the winter, and had an outside view of the celebrated or notorious Endowment House, where, as our driver said, "all the Mormon deviltry is concocted." This is an unpretentious, low stone house in the corner of a high-walled enclosure and has an innocent, modest, retiring look. The Bee Hive, where Brigham Young transacted the business of the great organization of which he was the ablest head, is a plain brick building and stands next the Lion House, so called from a gilded lion over the door, where he lived with a certain number of his many wives. The new Temple, now and for many years building, is far from complete. It is of a nondescript style of architecture, but will have the impressiveness belonging to bulk, with its walls a hundred feet high and nine feet thick, flanked with towers. The material is a beautiful white granite with specks of black.

In the evening attended a minstrel performance in a theatre of about the capacity, style of finish and ornament of the Brooklyn Theatre.

On the way to it a breeze sprang up, and all the air was full of dust—blinding, all-pervading. Through all this part of the world dust is one of the plagues, serious to strangers, and borne by the residents as a remediless evil.

## CHAPTER XIX.

*A beautiful morning—Attend service in the Congregational Church—Liberty of speech and some specimens—A visit to the Tabernacle—We describe its services, and make a few observations on polygamy and show how it can be abolished.*

*April 3d.*—Beautiful morning, mild and sunny, like our mid-May mornings. Attended a service in the Congregational Church, some sixty being present, a congregation fully up in appearance to those of towns of this size at the East. The clergyman seemed to think he had a call to speak of the town both in his prayer and sermon as a "sink of iniquity," a "rotten Gomorrah," etc. Our driver of yesterday used great license of speech relative to the Saints, saying, among other things, "We have got more'n a hundred of 'em in the Penitentiary and are hunting for more;" and a druggist, while preparing me a prescription, took time to give as answer to my question about the population of the city that there were resident therein "about five thousand people and twenty-five thousand beasts." One would infer that the Gentiles said their say in a city where they are not compelled to come, and where they are certainly not welcome; but their leading morning daily has an editorial this morning demanding, among other things, "more liberty of speech," and this on a page containing many "hard sayings" anent the Saints. One feels a languid interest in having this editor define "liberty of speech."

P.M. attended services in the Tabernacle, an enormous auditorium with a curved roof, like a turtle's upper shell, resting on outside pillars. The interior is plain to bareness, but admirably adapted to the meeting of the vast congregation of the Saints, having seats for twelve thousand. At one end stands a great organ, said to be the largest in the United States, manufactured here by Mormon workmen. Below this are ranged in degrees the various orders of the Mormon hierarchy, and before them stretches the vast expanse of the hall, with a wide gallery running round three sides. The acoustic properties are excellent, and the words of any one speaking in an ordinary tone of voice can be well heard anywhere in it. I estimate the congregation to-day at nine thousand. It was composed of the plainest and humblest folk, men and women gathered here from many lands out of the lower, if not lowest, walks of life at home, faces and forms where hereditary want and ignorance have set deep marks, and toil and care have worn away grace and beauty. They were of many nationalities, Norwegians, English, Welsh, Dutch, with a sprinkling of all others, not a great many Americans, and, I should say, fewest Irish of any.

It was communion day, and, standing before a long table, ten bishops took some time in breaking bread sufficient for so great a body of communicants ; and then, after a short blessing, asked in apt words by the oldest of the ten, a great number of young men were sent about with the holy emblem. Meanwhile a young elder had taken the preacher's desk, and now began a sort of "deliverance," speaking, as he said, according to the promptings of the Holy Spirit within him. Indeed, they have no regular and ordained clergymen for their stated services, but any one, be he of the priesthood or laity, is at liberty to "take up his testimony" when moved thereto by an inward impulse. The young man who now asked the attention of the hushed assembly began in a low tone, with humble manner and hesitating speech, but grew bolder as the Spirit gave him confidence, and after reciting some of the trials he had undergone as a missionary in some of the Southern States, he fervidly declared the triumph of the Church of Latter Day Saints to be nigh, and exhorted all his brethren to bear with patience and forbearance, yea with joy, the persecutions they must needs endure at the hands of the Gentile despisers of God and His true Church. He was followed by another young man in even a more fiery strain, to the same purpose; and when he had finished, after a blessing on the cup, in which was water and not wine, and this had been started on its way in many huge goblets, an older and more seasoned elder took the pulpit and set forth the main tenets of the Church, without once mentioning polygamy.

From him and elsewhere I gather that they are full believers in the inspiration of the entire Bible, that they are Trinitarians, believe in the Redemption—in brief, would be called orthodox by most of the dissenting churches, up to an advanced point. But beyond this, they hold, somewhat like the Irvingites and the so-called Catholic Apostolic Church, that in these latter times God is revealing Himself anew in fresh signs and wonders, as in the days of the early Church, and, more, that He has made a further revelation of His will in the Book of Mormon, that Joseph Smith was an inspired prophet, and that from his advent until now His will is revealed through the divinely chosen head of the Mormon Church. They also hold that polygamy, or a plurality of wives, is ordained, although this was not revealed in the Book of Mormon.

I was much entertained with the manner in which the last speaker used texts of Scripture to support his views, and found a fresh proof of the fact that almost any system of morals or faith can be bolstered by passages of the Bible, separated from the context. The Mormon teachers are dabsters at this sort of argument, are well versed in the Scriptures, and the Gentile must be well grounded and equipped at all points if he proposes to undertake a discussion with them; as the versatile and over-confident Rev. J. P. Newman found, when, in 1870, he cantered out here and discussed the question, "Does the Bible sanction Polygamy?" with the wily Orson Pratt.

The speakers to-day were narrow, illiterate men, and their labored reasonings from the Bible and their expositions of particular texts were dreary in the extreme, as all such preachments are from whatever pulpit, but their faith and trust in the tenets of their Church, and their zeal, equal to much suffering, if not martyrdom, was apparent. Meantime, what thoughts are in the minds of the silent bishops sitting in a row and apparently all intent on the preaching? They have the appearance of an able body of men, mentally and physically, and the worldly wisdom with which the temporal affairs of this great organization is conducted cannot be questioned.

As one sits in this great congregation of simple and confiding believers and looks on the strong faces of these spiritual and temporal rulers, it is difficult to believe that they are honest in professing to think that the Book of Mormon is a divine revelation or that the command to take more wives than one is not a priestly contrivance for the safe indulgence of lust. But who can fathom the human heart or fix limits to its credulity? Do we not constantly see men of superior minds honestly holding creeds and practices abhorrent to the average sense of mankind? Whether honestly or not, it is true that many of the heads of the Church and the more prosperous of the laity do have more than one wife. A great many houses were pointed out to me where it was said plural wives lived, each in her own establishment, and the names of several bishops and prominent leaders were given in connection with these—in one case to the number of eleven. I noticed that these particular domiciles were painted each a different color, and was told this is the custom, and affords the means of distinguishing them from each other. One can understand that a deeply bibulous Saint returning at a late hour to the domicile most likely to receive him leniently might find this distinction of color a convenience, but as they claim to have in all the city no drinking-place kept or frequented by Mormons, there must be some other reason for this diversity.

What happiness and what misery are in these alliances must to the outside world be largely a matter of conjecture ; but, as human nature is constituted and trained in nations of Saxon origin which have never tolerated polygamy, one cannot help thinking it a system of coarse degradation, especially to the women involved in it. It is said that most of these plural wives were poor, hard-working women with no prospects in life, to whom the shelter and protection afforded them by a well-to-do man, under the sanction of a sort of marriage, are sufficient to yield as much satisfaction in this life as they may hope for in any other way. But these relations will certainly not be permitted to continue. The indignation of the country is roused, and the clamor against polygamy, raised often by men whose own practices are equally blameworthy, is embodied in the Edmunds law now being vigorously enforced, and it is hard to see how the Saints can continue to bear up against the disabilities they are under.

It illustrates the constancy of woman that it

is rare for one of the wives to testify against her husband, so that bigamy is not so easily proven as one would expect. Still, a large number have been convicted and imprisoned and heavily fined. The wisest course would seem to be to abandon polygamy, which would settle the whole difficulty, and is easy to do, because as it was originally ordained by one special revelation so it may be abrogated by another. But, as always and everywhere, persecution only confirms belief among the persecuted, so that what was for the most part only a convenient practice becomes exalted into an article of faith held more and more tenaciously as afflictions increase by reason of it.

One cannot withhold a certain sympathy and pity for this people, who, having endured much for conscience' sake as we must think, are in danger of being driven from this goodly retreat, where, under a wise and just polity in many essential respects, they have thriven well, and, so far as this life at least is concerned, greatly benefited their condition.

There can be no question of the ability of Brigham Young as an organizer of men. He was a man of striking ability, and in ruder times, when individuality counted for more than now, and in a more superstitious age when Mahomets were possible, this strenuous Vermonter would have been a power in the world. He is buried in a plainly enclosed field of several acres, in a coffin said to be wide enough for him to turn and rest himself in his long sleep, for he gave it to be understood that he has only withdrawn himself from his followers for a term of years.

# CHAPTER XX.

*Leave Salt Lake City for Provo—Castle Gate and Cliffs—Pass through Gunnison and cross the Rocky Mountains—View the wonders of the Grand Cañon of the Arkansas—Manitou Springs —The " Garden of the Gods "—The grave of Helen Hunt—Denver—The mining regions— Meet with a railroad accident—A wait, when we have time to see the antics of a " bucking broncho" —Off again—Nearing home—Pleasant cogitations—Home at last.*

*April 4th.*—Left Salt Lake at 10 A.M. by the Denver and Rio Grande, going up the valley of the Jordan to the Mormon town of Provo, fifty miles south on the shore of the beautiful Lake Utah, and, turning eastward, follow the Spanish Fork and Clear Creek to Soldier Summit, a low pass in the southern part of the Wahsatch range. Provo, where we lunched, is forty-five hundred feet above the sea, and at Soldier Summit, forty-five miles beyond, the elevation is seventy-four hundred feet, or thirty-two hundred feet above Salt Lake City. There is notable scenery along the Spanish Fork Cañon, and at the summit of the pass, Mount Nebo, one of the loftiest peaks of the Wahsatch range, is seen to lift its snowy top twelve thousand feet high. Twenty-two miles from the top of the pass are remarkable cliffs, called the Castle Gate, forming the entrance to Castle Cañon, along which, on either hand, rise huge walls of red sandstone in startling likeness of castle walls with rounded towers and battlements, topped, in many instances, with layers of white sandstone, as if built by the skilful hands of giant masons.

Took supper at Green River, and,

*April 5th*, breakfasted at Cimarron and entered upon the famous Black Cañon of the Gunnison. For nine miles the road lies between steep, towering walls of rock from one to two thousand feet high. There are several transverse ravines coming in, with scarcely less imposing views, and frequent cascades. At one point of intersection of two gorges is a single detached tower called the Currecanti Needle, nearly a thousand feet high.

Passed through the mining town of Gunnison, and lunched at Sargent, then climbed the main range of the Rocky Mountains to Marshall Pass, 10,180 feet above the sea, the train being divided into two sections, each with two engines, as the grade in places is over two hundred feet to the mile. The train passes under nineteen long snow-sheds, said to cover forty miles of the track, before reaching the summit, where the track is also under cover, and in descending, at one point, after going five miles, the train is just opposite its former position and one thousand feet below it. The views, both up and down, are indescribably grand, including a near one of Mount Ouray, fourteen thousand feet high, the snowy domes of the Cochetopa range, from ten to thirteen thousand feet, and the lofty snow pinnacles of the Sangre de Cristo range. Reaching the bottom through the Pancho Pass, we come to Salida, a brand-new town of some three thousand population on the Arkansas River, with aspirations and a good hotel. We pass an uncomfortable night there in our Pullman-sleeper, and,

*April 6th*, after an early breakfast, enter on the wonderful scenery of the Grand Cañon of the Arkansas. Here is shown the prodigious power of water in shaping the configuration of the earth's surface, where lofty mountains of rock are cut sheer down a thousand feet by it. At a passage called the Royal Gorge there is not room enough for both stream and railway between the solid and almost perpendicular walls, and one side of the track is supported by rods hung to bars let into the rocks on both sides. Emerging from this awful chasm we come to Pueblo, a smart town of say twenty thousand population, where we lunch, and forty-five miles beyond reach Colorado Springs, whence a branch road conveys us to Manitou Springs and the Barker House, four miles away.

Besides its situation in a picturesque ravine of the Pike's Peak range—a spur of the Rocky Mountains—Manitou has celebrity from its soda springs, one of which is specially fine. A mile up a ravine is an iron spring of delicious water —soda impregnated with iron in agreeable proportions — cold as ice water. There are the hotels and cluster of stores and cottages usual to a young and promising watering-place. The mountains about are cut deeply with numerous cañons, and the drives are specially interesting. At the right of the entrance to the cañon where the village of Manitou nestles are remarkable forms of red sandstone remaining from the disintegration of a mountain, scattered in the most picturesque way over say a hundred acres, the whole taking the name of " The Garden of the Gods." Titanic shapes carved by nature's hand rise all about with startling likeness to the familiar works of man. The whole scene is weird and strangely phantasmal to the border of *diablerie* and leaves an impression not easily effaced.

We went up the Ute Pass to Manitou Grand Caverns, a narrow passage into the side of the mountain, which enlarges here and there into greater spaces, with lofty ceilings, sometimes domed, showing vast and mysterious in the dim light of the lamps. The stalactites are small and this cavern is insignificant in comparison with many others both in this country and in Europe. High up on a cliff of the Cheyenne Cañon is the grave of Helen Hunt, the gifted poet, whose burning spirit loved the cooling touch of nature here where she was wont to come both for labor and for rest.

*April 8th.*—Came to Denver by the Denver and Rio Grande Railroad, eighty-one miles. Good rooms at the Windsor. Denver is a well-built city of, as is claimed, seventy thousand population, has signs of present and future importance, but presents few objects to specially interest the visitor. It has one of the prettiest of theatres, where on Saturday evening we saw Robson and Crane in " Merry Wives of Windsor." The Windsor is an excellent hotel. The water used is from an artesian well, and I never used for drinking or bathing any I liked better.

The climate here is said to be mild and agreeable, although one mile above the sea-level. Some twelve miles to the westward extends from north to south for more than two hundred miles the Colorado range of the Rocky Mountains. Away to the south rises Pike's Peak over fourteen thousand feet, and to the northwest Gray's Peak, 14,440 feet, and between these two many another, the whole range presenting a scene of grandeur and beauty.

*April 11th.*—At 8 A.M. took the train on the Colorado Division of the Union Pacific up Clear Creek Cañon to Golden, Idaho Springs, Georgetown, and Silver Plume, a region abounding in mines of silver, with remains all along the creek of placer-mining. This is an old mining region, Georgetown being more than thirty years old. I shall hereafter have a more definite notion of what a man means when he says he owns a silver mine, and that most likely it is a small and nearly inaccessible hole in the side of a savage mountain with a glorious uncertainty of what can be found in it.

The mountain scenery all the way up to Georgetown is of the wildest and grandest. The road climbs up the steep ascents and rounds the abrupt curves in a manner abundantly testifying to the daring skill of the engineers who built it. At one place it parallels itself three times, crosses a bridge ninety feet high and makes a complete loop.

Returned to Denver and took the train on the Omaha and Denver Short Line of the Union Pacific for home direct, having supper on the same hotel-car we left at Ogden, the "International." When home again we should have made nearly twelve thousand miles by railroad, and I hoped we might say without any accident, for so far we had been spared the most trivial; but at four o'clock in the morning of

*April* 12*th*, as we were bowling along at a great rate, I was startled by a heavy bump, giving quite a shock, and then all was still except the lessening whistle of the engine. Our car was the last one of the long train, and I lay thinking that by some means it had become detached and was left standing on the track by the train whose receding whistle I was listening to as it tore away; but soon the report came that our engine had collided with another used in the yard at North Platte, where we were, wrecking both and killing the other engineer. It did not seem quite clear who was at fault, but it was pretty plain that he had not observed a telegram shown him and said to have been receipted for by him, that our train—a special—would be at the station at the moment it actually arrived. The two engines had struck each other fairly in the face and were badly damaged, both platforms of the baggage-car were crushed, without injury to the baggage itself, the forward platform of the first sleeper—the whole train was composed of these—somewhat damaged, and, what was of importance, since it deprived us of our meals aboard the car, the range of the "International" was so injured that no cooking could be done on it until it should go to the shop for repairs.

It was four hours before we were fitted to go on. Meantime we had breakfast at the station, and a chance to see a new thing to me—a "bucking broncho" ridden by a cowboy. A saddle was put on his back with some difficulty, firmly strapped, and the young fellow leaped easily to his seat, but not to rest at ease. After a moment of painful suspense the animal, small, compact and tough, reared straight into the air and stood on his hind legs for an instant, and then throwing his forefeet rapidly down to the ground, at the same instant flung his heels high into the air, and, with his nose well down between his legs, repeated these movements in alternation with such velocity that the different motions could scarcely be distinguished, and it seemed impossible that any rider could keep his seat. But this one sat like a centaur and allowed the broncho to exhaust all his tricks, and then plying a savage whip compelled him into a wild run all the way round an entire block of buildings, a distance of nearly a mile, and brought him to the stable in an apparently meek and fully subdued condition. But when he turned the broncho's head down the street for further exercise, the treacherous beast, as if all he had done before was mere prelude, instantly threw himself into a rapid series of convulsive twistings and contorted curvetings, ending by falling heavily in what looked from a distance like an attempted somersault, and both horse and man lay in a motionless heap. A cry rose among the spectators that the broncho had broken his neck and killed his rider, but after a few moments both horse and man were disentangled, and the cowboy, quite unhurt, led the now thoroughly humbled beast into his stable as coolly as if nothing had taken place out of the ordinary way.

A little before noon we moved on behind a fresh engine, traversing the level and fertile plains in the neighborhood of the Platte River, a region well watered, and capable, one would think, of great crops, and reached Omaha at dusk. We saw nothing of this prosperous city where we crossed the broad Missouri flowing darkly in the dull light to Council Bluffs. Thence on again without delay, all night long, over the Chicago, Rock Island and Pacific Railway, waking,

*April* 13*th*, in central Iowa, whose flat plains, abounding in fair streams and the moisture left by departing winter, showed soft in the near presence of full springtime, and went far to reconcile me to the sharp vicissitudes of our northern climate. At Blue Island Junction, seventeen miles from Chicago, we changed to the Chicago and Grand Trunk Railway, through South Bend, across Prairie Ronde, the home of my youth, quite wrapped in darkness, through Lansing to Port Huron, crossing the St. Clair River there, thence to London, Canada, where we breakfasted.

*April 14th.*—Reached Niagara Falls at 11 A.M. Passed several hours here admiring for the twentieth time with increasing awe this wonder, not eclipsed by anything we had seen in all our long journey among natural wonders. Home by West Shore Railway, running all night, and as, at waking, I lifted the curtain to my berth and looked out on the magnificent Hudson, whose waters and fair shores shone sweetly in the mild rays of the rising sun, it occurred to me that those who can live where are scenes like this are not altogether objects of pity even to the Southern Californian, whose "skies ever smile." Home to breakfast in Brooklyn, at 8 A.M., on 15th April, just as promised by the Itinerary, finding all well, but with doleful tales of "such an inclement spring as hardly ever was."

www.ingramcontent.com/pod-product-compliance
Lightning Source LLC
Chambersburg PA
CBHW032154160426
43197CB00008B/917